Educating America's Military

This book offers a detailed examination of the professional military education (PME) system in the United States, specifically the War Colleges, from a critical, insider's perspective.

The mission of America's War Colleges is to educate senior military officers in both the ways of war and the defense of peace. But are these colleges doing the best job possible in carrying out that important mission? Military education faces many demands, including a lack of preparation by the students, uneven quality of the faculty, and confusion over the goals of the curriculum. Some officers attend resident programs at the War Colleges against the career advice of their leadership, despite the fact that they are virtually guaranteed graduation after less than a year of study, while others do their best to avoid it entirely. As the professional military education system has come under increasing scrutiny and criticism, some have even called for closing the War Colleges. That answer, however, does not serve the United States well, especially in a complex, globalized environment, where military leaders need the best specialized education to prepare them for their future challenges. This volume examines the PME system, how it is perpetuated, and why it is imperative that it is fixed.

Written by a faculty member at a military college with 20 years' experience of the PME system, this book will be of much interest to students of the US Military, US politics and military education in general.

Joan Johnson-Freese is Professor of National Security Affairs at the Naval War College in Newport, Rhode Island. She served as department chair from 2002 to 2010, and has taught in Professional Military Education programs since 1993. She is also the author of several books on space security.

Cass Military Series

Educating America's Military

Joan Johnson-Freese

Routledge
Taylor & Francis Group

LONDON AND NEW YORK

First published 2013
by Routledge
2 Park Square, Milton Park, Abingdon, Oxon, OX14 4RN

Simultaneously published in the USA and Canada
by Routledge
711 Third Avenue, New York, NY 10017

Routledge is an imprint of the Taylor & Francis Group, an informa business

British Library Cataloguing in Publication Data
A catalogue record for this book is available from the British Library

Library of Congress Cataloging-in-Publication Data
Johnson-Freese, Joan.
Educating America's Military / Joan Johnson-Freese.
p. cm.
Includes bibliographical references and index.
1. Military education–United States. 2. Army War College (U.S.) 3. Naval War
College (U.S.) 4. National War College (U.S.) 5. Air University (U.S.) I. Title.
U408.3.J64 2013
355.0071'173–dc23
2012017480

978-0-415-63535-6 (hbk)
978-0-415-63499-1 (pbk)
978-0-203-07910-2 (ebk)

Typeset in Times by
FiSH Books Ltd, Enfield

Printed and bound in the United States of America by Publishers Graphics,
LLC on sustainably sourced paper.

Contents

Preface

Usually a preface is the author's short and personal introduction to a book and its subject matter, along with expressions of gratitude to the institutions and colleagues who have offered their assistance during the course of researching and writing it. I am pleased to have the opportunity to follow that tradition here.

This book is about Professional Military Education (PME), the process and institutions charged with providing post-enlistment education to most military officers. Specifically, it is about the most senior of those institutions, the War Colleges. PME brings together two important areas: national security and education. Both are central to America's strength and democratic tradition.

But I feel I also have to add a few words more about myself, why this book was written, and what I hoped to achieve with it. The reason for that is, quite frankly, that there is no way to write a book like this – which is critical of the institutional world in which I live and work – without having one's intentions called into question. In fact, I have already encountered some of these questions after I wrote the article, published in the Winter 2012 edition of *Orbis*, that was effectively the early draft of this book.

Many of my colleagues at the Naval, Army, and Air War Colleges, as well as at other professional military education institutions, supported a renewed and invigorated debate on the purpose and execution of military education. But some people also questioned my motives. Why was I critical of my colleagues? How could I judge the students harshly? Who was I to question the wisdom of the administrators and leaders above me? What "agenda" was I pursuing? What grudge was I nursing?

While it is somewhat unusual to discuss one's background as an author, the questions I've been asked – and questions that perhaps that you, the reader, might have – should be laid to rest before you continue reading this volume.

The truth is that I had nothing to gain from writing a book about professional military education. There is no further academic rank to which I can be promoted, and I have already been tenured on three separate occasions, including in my present position, in civilian and military academia. I am in the penultimate stage of a long and, if I may say, successful career spanning nearly 30 years. I have enjoyed a success beyond my own expectations and been treated quite well by the institutions I have served, even when I have disagreed with their practices.

I never really intended to write a book about PME – I already had an active research agenda in the field of space security. But when others began writing about their PME experiences, and were, in some cases, personally berated, and their critiques dismissed, I felt that I had an obligation to keep the discussion from being snuffed out. Moreover, I pursued the subject for two reasons.

First, I genuinely believe in the importance of what I have spent most of my career doing. I have stayed in PME because it is an institution crucial to the national defense of the United States. But I do believe the PME system could better and more effectively serve the national interest. I believe that informed and honest debate is central to military education and to a healthy civil–military relationship.

And second, I care very much about my students. I am acutely aware, especially in these dangerous days of war without end, that the men and women who sit in my classes are going to close their books at the end of the year, and then risk their lives for all of us. I have for years been aware of an inescapable and unsettling feeling that the PME system was not preparing America's warriors and future leaders as well as we might hope. To some extent, this book is offered as partial payment of a debt I feel I owe to them. They are giving us their best in the field, and we own them no less in the schoolhouses.

It is equally important to note some of the reasons I did *not* write this book. I did not seek to sow discontent or discord, except insofar as to produce better thinking about our duty as educators. Others, whom I cite in this book, have already written candid and, in some cases, understandably scathing memoirs. I had no intention of adding to that genre, but if some of my colleagues feel I was too harsh in my diagnosis of the current system, so be it. My goal, however, is to incite debate, not anger.

But there is no way around it. Some of the material in this book will produce, I suppose, hurt feelings or bruised egos, or even outright indignation. That is the nature of writing a critical analysis of any large organization. I hope, however, that this book will not be greeted with the most counterproductive emotion of all: denial.

Finally, I did not write this book for money. I am well-compensated as a senior faculty member at the nation's premier military school, and I do not need to fatten my bank account through this effort. And so to emphasize my deep respect for the sacrifices made by our students and military faculty when they take up arms on our country's behalf, I am donating any royalties due to me that may result from this book to the Wounded Warrior Project, with my sincere thanks to our veterans.

Many people from many institutions deserve thanks for the considerable assistance they gave me as I wrote this book. Individuals read and commented sometimes on multiple iterations of chapters and sections. Others shared their perspectives in person, in writing, on the phone, and via email. But because there is still considerable anxiety among the PME faculty about speaking out, many of my colleagues provided information and anecdotes on condition of anonymity, and so rather than single some out by name and others not, I wish to thank the group collectively. I cannot express my gratitude enough for the time and energy these individuals have spent helping me make this book what I hope will be a useful critique.

I also want to thank Colin Clark at *AOL.Defense* for giving me my first venue to write about PME. Similarly, the USNI blog gave me the opportunity to comment on my *AOL.Defense* articles discussed at that venue, and I would like to thank them for that courtesy. Also, I want to thank Mackubin Owens, Executive Editor of *Orbis*, for encouraging me to think through many of these issues at book length. Finally, I want to thank my friend Michael Kathrens, an accomplished writer and author in his own right, for reading the text to assure that it was understandable to the lay reader. Any remaining lapses into jargon are my fault, not his.

I have written a book that is partly a social-science effort and partly a journalistic enterprise, and even to some extent a memoir of my own career and experiences. I hope in the future more people will feel freer to speak out now that this book is complete. As I discuss at the close of the book, I hope that more scholars in PME and outside the system will come forward to produce more work, grounded in more data, to improve military education.

I also want to thank the long line of Naval War College presidents, and the current provost, Ambassador Mary Ann Peters, for their consistent and unwavering support of academic freedom. Obviously, this book would not have been possible otherwise. However, the conclusions and views in this book are *mine and mine alone*; they are not the views of the U.S. Government, the Navy, any other group I may be associated with, or any of the colleagues who provided assistance and criticism.

Finally, this book is dedicated to my father, Robert H. Johnson, who served in the U.S. Navy during World War II. He carried the pride of that service and patriotism for his country with him throughout his life.

List of abbreviations

AAR	After Action Report
AAUP	American Association of University Professors
ACSC	Air Command and Staff College
AWC	Air War College
CDE	College of Distance Education
CIST	Countering Ideological Support for Terrorism
CJCS	Chairman of the Joint Chiefs of Staff
CNWS	Center for Naval Warfare Studies
CO	Commanding Officer
DOD	Department of Defense
DSB	Defence Science Board
FEMA	Federal Emergency Management Agency
HASC	House Armed Services Committee
ICBM	Intercontinental Ballistic Missile
ILC	Intermediate Level Course (of JPME)
JPME	Joint Professional Military Education
NATO	North Atlantic Treaty Organisation
NDU	National Defense University
NEASC	New England Association of Schools and Colleges
NWC	Naval War College
OPMEP	Officer Professional Military Education Policy
PAJE	Process for Accreditation of Joint Military Education
PME	Professional Military Education
ROTC	Reserve Officers' Training Corps
SLC	Senior Level Course (of JPME)
TQM	Total Quality Management
QED	quod erta demonstrandum – "which was to be demonstrated"

1 Why War Colleges?[1]

Nail your whispers to the wall. Conclude the trilogy of read...think...and write. Is there 'career risk' in publishing? I suppose. Hasn't hurt me too badly over the years, I'd say. But what matters is testing your ideas on the field of intellectual battle, so to speak.

Admiral James Stavridis, Speaking at National War College Convocation ceremony, August 2011[2]

In September 2011, I appeared on the CSPAN television show *Washington Journal* to talk about Professional Military Education (PME), speaking from my near 20 years' experience as a PME faculty member, including as a former department chair and current professor at the Naval War College. A skeptical viewer called in with a question about why the United States needed *war* colleges...wouldn't we be better off having *peace* colleges? It is not an uncommon question and one I am always happy to answer. There is an inscription on the wall at the Naval War College, taken from the United Nations Educational, Scientific and Cultural Organization (UNESCO) charter, that sums up the answer well: "Since war begins in the minds of men, it is in the minds of men that defenses of peace must be constructed."

The caller's question points out though that few Americans are familiar with the Professional Military Education system either in terms of goals or processes. Yet it is through those institutions that most military members receive their post-enlistment training and education. It is within War Colleges that "the minds of men" are shaped to better construct "defenses of peace." The importance of these venerable institutions cannot be overstated, as it is here that American military officers should prepare to transition from operational leaders – those proficient in battlefield skills and tactics, to strategic leaders – those responsible for decisions at higher and broader levels.

With inevitable Defense Department budget cuts looming, all programs will be scrutinized, especially those not directly related to war fighting. War Colleges are too important to be considered low-hanging fruit. Consequently, it is imperative that decision-makers understand their importance, and that the institutions are able to demonstrate rigor and they are serving the purpose for which they were intended.

Therefore, the purpose of this book is twofold: to familiarize the American public and decision-makers with PME, specifically the senior War Colleges, and to encourage discussion on how to improve the execution of their important missions. The latter purpose stems from the idea that there is always room for improvement. Before improvement can take place, though, the goals must be clear. But whether War College goals are clear, and whether articulated goals are then supported by practices and processes at those institutions, is part of this discussion.

Admiral James Stavridis provided a succinct articulation of his view on War College educational goals at the 2011 National War College Convocation by describing his own situation when he arrived at National in 1991.

> I knew what I was good at and what I knew well: driving a destroyer or a cruiser; navigating through tight waters; leading a boarding party up a swinging ladder; planning an air defense campaign; leading Sailors on the deck plates of a rolling ship. But I also sensed what I did not know or understand well: global politics and grand strategy; the importance of the "logistics nation"; how the interagency community worked; what the levers of power and practice were in the world – *in essence, how everything fits together in producing security for the United States and our partners.* [emphasis added][3]

The goal of the War Colleges should be to educate students in the areas they are not familiar with and take them out of their comfort zones. War College students are senior military officers who are transitioning from career positions where tactical (often technical) skills are key – flying planes, driving ships, leading infantry – to positions requiring a broader view of the role of the military in U.S. security affairs, including areas of a non-technical, non-kinetic nature.

Global politics and grand strategy, as Admiral Stavridis states, are areas with which War College students are largely unfamiliar, but areas for which some will be responsible in their future positions, and others will support. Too often, though, educational achievement in those areas is diluted, sacrificed for expedience at the nation's War Colleges. That being the case, America is neither getting what it is paying for with the millions – billions?[4] – annually spent on our nation's War Colleges, nor preparing its military leaders both to fight wars and construct defenses for peace. Admittedly, the broad range of War College students' interests, abilities, intellectual bent, future jobs and missions, and the unique constraints of the military profession, creates challenges in Professional Military Education not evident at civilian schools. It also makes it even more important to be continually striving for improvement. Professional Military Education serves an array of purposes, through multiple institutions at varying levels, with War Colleges at the pinnacle for most officers.[5]

As part of the PME system, War Colleges are a large complex of institutions modeled on universities. They include the Army War College in Carlisle Barracks, PA; the Naval War College in Newport, RI; the Air War College in Montgomery, AL; the Marine Corps War College in Quantico, VA; the National War College in Washington, D.C.; and the Industrial College of the Armed Forces (ICAF), also located in Washington, D.C.[a] Each institution has a distinct personality and individual strengths and weaknesses.

Professional Military Education, in general, includes training and education provided to military members by the military along what is known as an education continuum.[6] It includes opportunities for enlisted personnel and officers in their specialty fields, as well as offering Bachelor's degrees at the service academies and Master's degrees at some staff colleges and all the War Colleges, and Master's and doctoral degrees at the Air Force Institute of Technology and at the Naval Post Graduate School. The focus of this book is at the War College level, specifically the Army, Navy, Air Force, and National

a   The Air War College is part of Air University. National War College and ICAF are part of the National Defense University.

War Colleges,[b] because it is there that senior officers focus on the things they do not know or understand well; non-technical, broadly focussed issues.

While all of these institutions excel in some or many areas, all also suffer to varying degrees from overriding institutional and cultural issues that hinder the education goals intended by Congress, and codified in the 1986 Goldwater-Nichols Act. Goldwater-Nichols was landmark legislation that fundamentally reformed U.S. national defense. It was intended to address issues created by inter-service rivalry that hindered U.S. operations in Vietnam, the Iranian hostage rescue mission in 1980,[7] and Grenada in 1983.

> In an engagement [Grenada] where U.S. military superiority was absolute, the interoperability of U.S. forces proved shocking poor. Communications between the Services was poor, if not non-existent in some cases, leading to deadly situations for U.S. forces as well as sheer redundancy of effort in an era where the United States could afford redundancy.[8]

The services needed to work better together, and Grenada finally provided the impetus for Congress to legislatively force "jointness" amongst the services through Goldwater-Nichols.

Goldwater-Nichols streamlined the military chain of command, strengthened the office of the Chairman of the Joint Chiefs of Staff (CJCS), and mandated that the services learn to work together, jointly, through combined/joint schooling. None of that would prove easy because of the high degree of military service insularity, or stovepiping, found historically. Beyond having the services learn to work with each other, part of Goldwater-Nichols also specifically mandated expanded guidelines for military education to open the military culture and to encourage intellectual integration with civilians and among the services themselves. That was prompted by military officers increasingly being left out of strategy and policy discussions because they did not have the capability to contribute from a knowledgeable position. They were good at what they did, but they had lost any sense of context.

---

b The Marine War College is not part of the focus as it is the youngest (established in 1990) and smaller than the other War Colleges.

Goldwater-Nichols was followed by the 1987 creation of a Panel on Military Education of the House Armed Services Committee, also known as the Skelton Panel after its chair, Ike Skelton (D-MO). Mr. Skelton believed that a strong joint educational system and effective personnel management practices had to be developed by the services in order to assure the "jointness" mandated by Goldwater-Nichols.[9] The idea behind both was simple, reflecting the classic wisdom that "the society that separates its scholars from its warriors will have its thinking done by cowards and its fighting done by fools."[10] The military must be included in strategy and policy discussions. Military education was to be significantly broadened beyond the traditional "operations" focus of the past, to include subjects important for context. This necessitated adding more civilian academics to War College faculties to cover substantive areas beyond the scope of the largely military faculty of previous years, and Goldwater-Nichols paved the way for that.

Over a decade earlier, Admiral Stansfield Turner had similarly reformed the Naval War College (NWC). In his 1972 Convocation address, Turner stated that reform was needed because: "Rarely does one meet a graduate of any War College who said that he had been intellectually taxed by a War College course of instruction."[11] He further warned in that speech that military officers must be able to hold their own with "the best civilian strategists or we will abdicate control over our profession."[12] Thus, in the 1970s, as the Naval War College President, he instituted what has become known as the Turner Revolution.

Admiral Turner reorganized the basic curriculum of the Naval War College into three blocks, reinstating strong foundational theory and history components that had been weakened in the years since Naval War College founder Stephen B. Luce and strategist/lecturer Alfred Thayer Mahan had presided.[13] Turner also significantly increased the number of civilian faculty that, according to Frederick Hartmann, former Alfred Thayer Mahan Chair of Maritime Studies and Special Academic Advisor to the President of the Naval War College, was "a more important change than the so-called 'revolution' in the curriculum."[14] Together, these two reforms were intended to enable military officers to be capable and competitive strategists by expanding the scope of military education beyond its natural inclination toward technical skill sets.

A key part of that Turner and Goldwater-Nichols military education revolution was to move military education away from what Samuel Huntington, in *The Soldier and the State*, had earlier called the "technicism" – concentration on a technical specialty – prominent in military culture.[15] Technicism, however, is what the services were and are largely comfortable with and want; and understandably so, given the increasing military reliance on increasingly sophisticated and complex technology. Consequently, the expanded subject matter and accompanying civilian academics legislatively thrust upon the War Colleges by Goldwater-Nichols have often been seen by military leadership as peripheral to service needs. But, as the war on terrorism has vividly demonstrated, technology cannot provide the answer to all questions.

Whether the intent of Goldwater-Nichols, the Skelton Panel and even the Turner Revolution has been upheld is debatable. Naval War College professor Mackubin Owens suggested in 2006 that it has not:

> I have heard too many Navy officers gloat about the "end of the Turner Revolution." The new mantra has become "teaching to competencies," which suggests the purpose of military education – to broaden the intellectual and military horizons of officers to encompass larger strategic and operational issues that will confront them in the future – has been abandoned for mere training.[16]

In 2009, the Secretary of Defense requested the Defense Science Board to conduct a review of PME, resulting in a major report.[17] That report referenced yet another study, this one authored in 2008 by defense analyst Barry Watts.[18]

> Watts argued that the military needs to develop strategists either by better educating officers or by institutionalizing a place for strategists to live. Both of these efforts are ultimately doomed to fail and neither for malicious reasons. The first is illustrated by the fact that our professional military education (PME) system believes that it is educating strategists/leaders. In fact, the curriculum normally reflects the flavor of the day; it is not necessarily aimed at selected critical thinkers but at officers who show acumen at following directions and who pass through the right jobs to get promoted. Moreover, staff college and War College attendees are deemed future leaders not by any scientific method, but by an inconsistent evaluation by senior leaders. Furthermore, school attendance is

viewed more as a "rite of passage" than a serious and rigorous honor that few are given access to, and where they are expected to perform at a higher academic level...

Beyond whether or not the students were being given the right material at the right level to prepare them as future strategic leaders, rather than better tactical or operational leaders, the DSB authors also addressed programmatic rigor.

Finally, the very dirty and not so secret truth is that majors [O-4 rank] in PME today are the products of an educational system in which many colleges and universities no longer hold students to the standard of being able to write coherent, logical arguments. An informal survey among Air University academics reveals that it is even worse today than in 1996, when Foster[19] said War College students did not write well and were "victims of a system that prizes decidedly non-objective advocacy." This truth cannot be overstated. It is little different from the national studies showing college graduates not being able to write paragraphs or form cogent arguments. If Air Force senior leaders read a sample of even top-tier majors' ACSC papers, they would be appalled at the students' inability to read through a problem, think through it, and write a solution.[20]

These articles and official reports presented a consensus view that PME could do better. Subsequently, this consensus was confirmed by a full review of PME in the context of Goldwater-Nichols mandates by the House Armed Services Committee (HASC).

In 2010, the House Armed Service Committee issued a report titled *Another Crossroads? Professional Military Education Twenty Years after the Goldwater Nichols and the Skelton Panel.* The panel focussed on the need for education toward intellectual agility, quite different to technical competency.

...the current PME system should be improved to meet the country's needs of today and tomorrow...PME, therefore, must remain dynamic. It must respond to present needs and consistently anticipate those of the future. It must continuously evolve in order to imbue service members with the *intellectual agility* to assume expanded roles and to perform new missions in an ever dynamic and increasingly complicated security environment. [emphasis added][21]

HASC went on to caution that many PME institutions were too focussed on technical education and tactical skills[22] – on training rather than education.

The HASC Report cites a 2005 study by Dr. Jeffrey McCausland, stating:

> ...the McCausland Study, reinforced by the Subcommittee's observations, pointed out the problem with having both deans and [Chief Academic Officers]: "each college should also have a single senior officer or civilian educator serving as both Dean and Provost to underscore the point that education, not training *du jour*, is the fundamental imperative of its institutional mission.[23]

Several key points are raised in this quote. The first is that education, not training, should be the goal of the War Colleges. Second, organizationally there is significant room for improvement among and within the War Colleges. Clearly there is, though reorganization alone will not suffice. In fact, reorganization is sometimes used as a substitute for real change. Whether or not, however, a "senior service officer or civilian educator" would be equally effective, indeed interchangeable, toward achieving the educational goals of Goldwater-Nichols, has been increasingly questioned. Senior service officers and civilian educators are from very different cultures. Those cultural differences are central among the issues being raised by individuals concerned about whether PME is really focussed on education rather than training.

Raising questions

Recently, the goals of, and methods used at, the War Colleges have been questioned by individuals who currently teach, or have taught, at those institutions, as well as external critics. George Reed, a retired Army officer who spent six years as Director of Command and Leadership Studies at the Army War College, and is currently a faculty member at the University of San Diego, has called it "a cascade of withering criticism."[24] Besides Reed, former Air War College professor Dan Hughes,[25] noted Latin America scholar and former National War College professor Howard Wiarda,[26] current Naval War College professor Mackubin Owens,[27] former Army War College commandant, Major General (retired) Robert Scales,[28] former visiting Army War College professor Judith Hicks Stiehm,[29] Army War College veteran colonel (retired) Charles Allen,[30] journalist Tom Ricks,[31] and I are among those who have published articles, books, or commentary raising issues regarding PME.

Judith Hicks Stiehm provides a relatively early discussion and analysis of the post-Cold War Army War College program in her 2002 book *The U.S. Army War College: Military Education in a Democracy*. While promoting the continued value of the institution, she nevertheless questions the school's pedagogy, declaring that, in many ways, the Army War College is more successful with training than with education.[32] She states:

> When the war-college year is measured against the ideal civilian education, it falls short. This needs to be recognized if the goal is in fact education rather than training. Let us assume that the goal of education is to stimulate individuals to habitual, critical, and creative thinking.[33]

Tom Ricks entered the general fray about PME in 2009 when he published "Why We Should Get Rid of West Point" (and the other service academies) in the *Washington Post*.[34] He concluded that while some graduates reminded him of "the best of the Ivy League," too often students were getting "community-college educations" at costs twice as expensive as civilian schools. Others have written about the service academies as well. Elizabeth D. Samet's *Soldier's Heart*[35] and Bruce Fleming's *Annapolis Autumn*[36] are both written from the perspective of long-time English department faculty members at West Point and Annapolis, respectively, and provide glimpses into the strengths and weakness – and hearts – of the academies.

Ricks then joined into the War College discussion in response to the piece written by Dan Hughes, which painted an unflattering picture of the Air War College (AWC). Professors were depicted as unqualified, coddled students, and the entire enterprise largely a waste of time. I also taught at the Air War College, and my five-year tenure in the 1990s overlapped with Dr. Hughes'. While personal experiences vary, mine was similar to his.

Most of those writing about PME have tried to discuss the problems, rather than comprehensively consider fixes, with the idea that dialog must precede answers. Ricks, however, at one time advocated closing the Air War College on his well-read blog,[37] a position with which I strongly disagree; but the frustration shown by Ricks and others with the inertia of the PME system is understandable.

General David Petraeus, the former commander of U.S. forces in Iraq and Afghanistan, and later CIA Director, has weighed in also. Petraeus, who graduated in the top 20% of his class at West Point and was the top graduate of the U.S. Army Command and Staff College, was considered by the Army (and himself) as a smart guy. Attending Princeton from 1983 to 1985 as a doctoral candidate in international relations was, however, according to Petraeus, an intellectual wake-up call.

> I certainly found my own experience at grad school to be quite humbling at times – starting with the "D" I got on my first advanced micro-economics exam. This frankly surprised me, for I went to grad school following a year at the Army's Command and General Staff College, during which I won the so-called "white briefcase." I stood first in our class of a thousand or so students, so as I entered grad school I believed I was a reasonably thoughtful fellow. The econ exam was followed quickly by a comment by Professor Richard Ullman, who was also the editor of *Foreign Policy* magazine at the time and eventually became my dissertation adviser, on a paper I wrote for him: "Though this paper is reasonably well written and has some merit, it is relatively simplistic," he observed, "and I am left feeling that the whole is less than the sum of the parts."[38]

Competing in this new environment not only imparted a degree of intellectual humility, but it also in the end prepared him to be not just a top military thinker, but also to compete with the best and the brightest anywhere.

Petraeus suggested that civilian schools were perhaps the proper venue for further officer education. That, however, is not a viable approach because of the specific substantive and "joint" requirements of Goldwater-Nichols[c] (not available at most civilian academic institutions)

---

c For example, toward creating more "joint" fighting force, military education must include specific percentages of members from each of the services in the student body.

and because of the sheer volume of military officers involved. Further, as George Reed states: "a top tier university would, in many respects, be a poor substitute for what *should* happen at War Colleges" [emphasis added].[39] Retired Army Lt. Colonel Ralph Peters challenged General Petraeus, castigated War College curricula, rejected the value of civilian education, and was particularly venomous in his tone regarding civilian academics:

> The last formal phase of in-house officer education is the War College, where largely civilian faculties instruct colonels and lieutenant-colonels on the countless theories academics have devised for avoiding war. Failed theories of international relations form the core curriculum... Perhaps the most perverted romance of recent decades (Lord knows, that's quite a low standard) is the love affair between the military and civilian academics. I challenge any reader to cite a single example of a social science professor's work contributing to any military victory...You should never let any full-time university professor near any form of practical responsibility, and you should never let a rising officer near a professor.[40]

Peters asserts soldiers and sailors get far more from training and experience than they ever will from education. However, Lt. Col. Peters appears to have made his assessment about the War College curricula without any recent or substantive basis for such. Having been part of the curriculum development and execution process for many years, at least at the Naval War College, it is not based on "countless theories academics have devised for avoiding war" and "failed theories of international relations."

Further, it is absurd to suggest that a senior officer will be more successful if they do not understand the context and processes of their operating environment, including Congress, domestic politics, international affairs, governance and societies of allies and competitors, the media and more. In fact, failed leaders have often failed because they did not understand the political or social ramifications of their actions. MacArthur's misreading the Chinese in Korea, Westmoreland thinking he could win a war of attrition in Vietnam, and failing to plan for reconstruction in Iraq and Afghanistan are among many errors in judgment that can be cited as rooted in failure to understand the environment.

More recently, Army General Stanley McChrystal's tenure as Commander, International Security Assistance Force (ISAF) and Commander, U.S. Forces Afghanistan (USFOR-A) exemplifies the need for more than operational bravado to succeed. His August 2009 "Initial Assessment of Afghanistan"[41] was peppered with suggestions regarding changing organizational cultures, better integration with Afghan forces and connecting with the people; all things inherently desirable (what is the counterargument, not to better integrate?) and all also inherently difficult, with little depth of understanding regarding the challenges evidenced. As one Army veteran of two tours in Afghanistan put it, "It briefed well." One could also cite McChrystal's apparent naivety about the motives of a *Rolling Stone* reporter "hanging out with" McChrystal and his staff – and the resultant damning article[42] – as directly resulting in McChrystal's career being cut short. A broader understanding of issues and interests might have served him, and the nation, better.

While Peters is by no means alone in his disdain for education and academics, he is perhaps the most vocal. In some respects, his honesty about his views is a welcome change from the pretense of acceptance that sometimes prevails in the War Colleges and from military leadership. At the Naval War College, a defense industry engineer-businessman turned top Navy and DOD official spoke to the faculty. He stated that unless regulations were lifted that required successful industry leaders to divest themselves of stock holdings raising potential conflict-of-interest issues before entering government service, there would be no top people in government, and government would be left to *academics* (said with great derision in his voice).

A view from the inside

When Michael Brown left FEMA, he wrote a scathing book called *Deadly Indifference: The Perfect (Political) Storm: Hurricane Katrina, The Bush White House, and Beyond.*[43] The kindest critics called it just another Washington tell-all, typical of any that could be written about any Washington bureaucracy. Some critics will undoubtedly place this book in that same genre.

Professional Military Education (PME) is part of the largest of all the Washington bureaucracies, the Department of Defense (DOD), and so, one can argue, inherently riddled with incompetence, politics, and waste. I would counter, however, that FEMA employees do not represent the United States of America in many corners of the world, carry weapons, or bear responsibility for the nuclear codes; (nor can FEMA employees, or any other federal employees except the military, retire in their mid-40s and immediately take another government job while also drawing a full pension). DOD is not only the largest, most heavily funded Washington bureaucracy, but it is also different in its responsibilities, thereby warranting both closer scrutiny and less tolerance for failing in any mission it takes on. Education is the mission of PME. Significant taxpayer dollars are spent to accomplish the mission, and PME is riddled with the worst problems of military bureaucracy as well as the worst attributes of civilian academia.

Howard Wiarda based his memoir of the National War College on several years' experience teaching at that institution in the 1990s. He found the institution burdened with policies and processes often not just arbitrary but also counterproductive toward the educational mission. Cynthia Watson, Chair and Professor of the Department of Security Studies at the National War College, where she has held positions since 1992, provides a very different description of the environment in a 2010 Army publication, *A Vision of Developing the National Security Strategist from the National War College.*[44] She describes National as an institution that is largely smoothly running, efficient, and effective. But it, too, is an anecdotal assessment. Watson states, for example, that NDU military faculty are "recruited at the 25-year mark in their careers"[45] but without a reference for that data point (which counters the perspectives and experience of others, including myself, who indicate that military faculty are assigned, not recruited). Wiarda and Watson make different assessments, and both can't be right.

Watson does say: "No one at the National War College is arrogant enough to believe that the process of educating strategists cannot be improved; it can and should be." She suggests, however, that constant internal assessment of subject matter and processes for "evaluating content, pedagogical techniques, readings, speakers, educational technology, and the outcomes of teaching"[46] are the mechanisms for improvement. The problems chronicled by Wiarda, however, include those very processes. If the problems chronicled by Wiarda from the 1990s at National – which I argue are endemic to the War Colleges generally – have been addressed, it will be helpful to others to learn, specifically, how, and only through open dialogue will that occur.

Even 10 or 15 years ago, criticisms of PME were basically taboo. Self-contained Brigadoons that only appeared in the DOD world briefly and irregularly, the War Colleges could ignore the isolated critical argument or book. Civilian academic faculty members were still few and no faculty member or student would risk retribution by raising criticism. Many PME faculty and staff will be reluctant, even now, to admit any contention or institutional problems, including for reasons of self-protection. Most individuals writing critically about PME issues are retired or, like myself, have one of a few effectively tenured positions. War College academic faculty are most often on two- to four-year contracts, and their pay is not in addition to a military pension. They fear retribution if they are not regarded as "team players" – a deadly accusation in the military world; and make no mistake: individuals fear retribution in any government job for raising unwanted criticism – that's why there are whistle-blower laws.

Bruce Fleming wrote about a two-tiered admission standard at Annapolis based on his years of service on the admissions committee in a 2010 *New York Times* editorial titled "The Academies' March Toward Mediocrity."[47] He argued that the academies needed to be "fixed or abolished." Subsequent to that editorial, Fleming alleged that he was denied a raise as retaliation, a claim validated by investigators from the U.S. Office of Special Counsel, and the Naval Academy was ordered to pay Fleming a settlement.[48] As a critic, his motives and assertions seem therefore to have become inherently suspect.

A review of his 2010 book, *Bridging the Military–Civilian Divide: What Each Side Must Know about the Other and about Itself*[49] in the Naval Institute publication *Proceedings* specifically suggests that Fleming might be "settling scores" in parts of the book. It further suggests that "Fleming's targets might have a different, but equally valid, perspective on events."[50] That is undoubtedly true, and one would expect invalid or untrue assertions to be refuted; but that does not seem to have happened.

Tom Ricks found himself "blackballed" by the Army War College because of his coverage of the Iraq War. Specifically, he was made aware of a 2005 email from Professor Steve Metz, a department chair at the Army's Strategic Studies Institute, encouraging faculty to "avoid Tom [Ricks] like the plague." Metz later explained to Ricks that his email had been prompted by the "political climate" at the Army War College at the time. Beyond the issues concerning himself, Ricks questioned whether Army War College faculty had curtailed their criticism of the Iraq War in fear of retaliation.[51]

Unfortunately, too, there are attempts to simply invalidate discussion by discrediting those who raise it. Air War College professor Dan Hughes suffered such an attack in a widely distributed email, eventually published as part of a United States Naval Institute blog article:

> The whine from the Air Force civilian professor that made the rounds recently suggested to me, after looking at his vita, that he probably couldn't get a research university job, "settled" for the Air Force institution and never quite grasped the mission – and for some time too. More broadly, to some extent this may be explained by the second-tier status of some significant number of civilian faculty at JPME institutions, who, at least some of them, evidently could not gain tenured positions in mainstream academia, and yet yearned for some semblance of that life.[52]

Not only does this kind of *ad hominem* attack on a PME colleague reinforce the stereotype of civilian professors as layabouts who "don't get it," but it is also a criticism that itself sounds resentful and angry. Tenure at a research university is elevated to the highest rank of credibility by implying that never gaining it, for whatever reason, is an immediate disqualification for speaking out about PME issues. Having tenure, however, could likely lead to one being labeled oblivious to the military mission – creating a Catch-22 where civilians who had tenure are clueless and those who did not are just bitter – with the inevitable result that only a select few initiates of the PME world can speak to the mission without their reputations being attacked.

A new factor that allows issues regarding PME to be raised for discussion is that online websites give individuals the platform to quickly disseminate critiques. There are venues to voice opinions. Several such opinions are cited in this book, written on blogs or websites by individuals, some of whom have chosen to remain anonymous or write under a pseudonym. Personally, I am grateful that the Naval War College has understood that the intent of discussion, such as has been generated by my online and print publications on PME, is toward open, transparent discussion and mission improvement.

I am fortunate to have far more data and specific information available to me than most faculty, from personal files, meeting memos, and various sources through my years as a department chair. Working with faculty and student demographic information, recruitment and hiring processes, curricula and broader institutional policy were part of my job. Nevertheless, I am also primarily reliant on experience on which to base my assertions, like Wiarda, Hughes, Fleming and others. As a scholar, I would prefer to be able to back all assertions with reliable data, but instead must adopt something more akin to a journalistic standard where statements are backed by at least two sources. I would expect, as well, that if I am incorrect in assertions that can be corrected by data – such as a near 100% graduation rate among War College students each year – those corrections would be offered by others. But I would point out that many of the assertions raised in this book were earlier raised in a Winter 2011 article in *Orbis*, "The Reform of Military Education: Twenty Five Years Later," and have not been refuted.

Being reliant on experience, I am also, rightfully, bound by the policy of non-attribution critical to open discussion within the War College. No names are used in conjunction with substantive discussions, unless they were made on the record, or with permission being given. While that can be suggested to further weaken the veracity of statements made, I would argue that it is policies and processes in general that are important for discussion.

This work is offered as a critique on an important niche in higher education. Because that niche is within the military, there will, inherently, also be considerations of civil–military relations, as well as aspects of an organizational culture study. There will likely be parts that come across as a tell-all, but hopefully those parts will be considered to have a purpose, rather than being more sensationalism.

Returning to the point about data; I offer now a preview from the final chapter on recommendations. Data currently available about PME institutions is largely gathered through self-studies. But there is always, inherently, skepticism about self-reported data used in assessments; understandably, no organization deliberately makes itself look bad, and in fact will shape data advantageously. There are two issues involved in gathering *useful* data: knowing the right questions to ask, and having the authority to request the data and have it provided in a timely, accurate and complete manner. Data gathered based on those two premises is lacking.

Therefore I strongly support the idea that a study needs to be produced by an organization with the mandate and the authority to ask probing questions and receive full answers, which then provides reliable, citable data on PME. In fact, that is my number-one recommendation for how to proceed with a useful, productive discussion toward improvement. It is my hope that this book will assist in the development of *appropriate questions* to ask in the gathering of data in the future.

Road map

This examination continues with a consideration of the differing military and academic cultures in Chapter 2. If the military has a proclivity toward technicism, as Huntington and others have argued is the case, then a proclivity toward training is not surprising. Machinery is neither built nor fixed by thinking about it; somebody has to *do* something, something that will have a right and wrong way to achieve the goal. But conceptualizing the need for, or employment of, that machinery – often in combination with human factors and considerations – is a different capability. The academic culture promotes critical thinking and open-ended questions and is associated with understanding a larger context – capabilities achieved through education. Both of these goals, and approaches toward achieving them, breed cultural norms.

The hybrid nature of PME institutions inherently brings together the military and academic cultures. With balance, the combination can create a healthy tension that results in an especially productive learning environment for America's military or, without balance, a counterproductive clash of cultures, to the ultimate detriment of the students and the nation. Which way the pendulum will swing is largely a function of guidance and follow-through toward goal achievement from military leadership, and execution through PME institutional leadership.

My position is that guidance and follow-through support from the military is lacking, and so the education provided to War College students is not what it could be, or needs to be. How that plays out for the students is the subject of Chapter 3, which looks at who attends war colleges and what is expected of them. Leaders and professionals in their operational careers, they have become the military equivalent of "too big to fail" in their educational requirements, as reflected by programs designed for all to succeed, and quickly. Consider as you read: How would you feel as a parent if your son or daughter asked you to pay somewhere between $57,000–166,000 (the range of "cost per student" at the War Colleges[53]) for him or her to attend a graduate program where there are no academic admission standards and *everyone* graduates in 10 months? (Unless the War Colleges are the military equivalent of the mythical Lake Wobegon, where all the children are above average, statistically, everyone graduating from an accelerated, rigorous graduate program where there are no admissions standards is highly unlikely.) Further, this program will constantly pulse your child to make sure he or she is "happy" with what they are being taught, by a faculty some of whom have neither teaching experience nor subject matter expertise. You might have qualms about the educational value of the program.

Chapter 4 looks at the PME faculty: active-duty military, retired military, academics, security practitioners, with many differentiations, strengths and weaknesses within each of those general groups. Representation is needed from all, though how many and in what capacity is a question I posit as needing serious reconsideration. Currently, PME faculty are hired on short, renewable contracts, which makes it virtually impossible for anyone to question institutional policies focussed on creating and executing a curriculum that is, theoretically, teachable by anyone, with the aim of graduating everyone. These policies are developed and enforced by a steadily growing number of administrators with no prior experience in scholarly activity, faculty management or mentorship, or curriculum development – sometimes not even in teaching.

Learning occurs in PME institutions, but more haphazardly than it ought to, and not necessarily in the areas that these individuals will need for the rest of their careers. Chapter 5 looks at what is taught and how – in theory and in practice. The curricular issues considered in this chapter link back to issues regarding faculty, institutional goals, and culture. A holistic look at the issues must be considered; there are no easy fixes.

Chapter 6 offers recommendations for how to begin removing the obstacles to providing our military leaders with more education and less training at the critical junctures of their careers when they are transitioning from operational to strategic positions. The knowledge, experience and skills that served them well at the tactical and operational levels are necessary but not sufficient for the remainder of their careers, in positions where some of them will be advising, or even making decisions for, the nation at large. If the nation expects greatness in our military leaders, it is the nation's responsibility to provide them with the education required to work effectively with the civilian peers whom they will inherently encounter in their future careers.

Twenty-five years after Goldwater-Nichols, the U.S. military operates in the most complex environment it has ever faced. The 2010 HASC review concluded that while improvements have been made, America could do better in effectively educating military officers for the future environment. In order to do that, however, there must be agreement on the educational goals to be achieved as well as processes and practices put in place and vigorously executed toward achieving those ends. That strategic alignment has not happened.

2 Warriors and scholars

Even a dysfunctional culture, once well established, is astonishingly efficient at reproducing itself.

Megan McArdle, *The Atlantic*, March 2012, p.31

There have been calls to simply close the War Colleges and send military officers to civilian schools. That is neither feasible nor desirable. There is simply not enough room for all the officers mandated to get further education in the very short time allotted for such in the elite schools, and so if sent to civilian schools many will end up in mediocre ones. They might well end up taking boutique courses like "Race, Gender and Class in American Political Thought," "Reformation History," "Republicanism and the Good Society," and "Occupy Everywhere" – all real courses and perhaps all relevant to individuals interested in particular subjects, but not relevant to military practitioners.

If education for our military leaders is valued, then the War Colleges must remain open and must strive to be among the best graduate programs in the nation. When officers who have the choice of attending a graduate program at Harvard, Yale, Columbia or any of the schools that would be the first choice of the best and brightest civilians, and instead they *choose* to attend one of the War Colleges, the War Colleges will have achieved success. There is considerable room for improvement if that goal is to be reached, and many obstacles along the way. The first of those obstacles is a failure in the military to distinguish between training and education.

Training versus education

Neither the DOD Joint Staff responsible for PME nor the individual military services have seriously tackled what education for intellectual agility (per the 2010 HASC report), as opposed to training, actually entails. That is not surprising, because few of those responsible for PME (individually or collectively) have spent much time thinking about the difference between education and training, or even what it means to be "educated", as their own careers have emphasized training; and so, unfortunately, training and education are often seen by the military bureaucracy as almost synonymous.[1]

When training and education are viewed interchangeably, intellectual agility becomes sacrificed to training-friendly metrics. During my first years as a Naval War College department chair, for example, the academic departments were asked more than once to provide metrics for "return on investment" for the Navy, in order to justify shortening the course, to speed up "throughput" of students, and to develop a curriculum teachable by virtually anyone.[2] If training courses can run from 0800 to 1700 five days a week, we were asked, why can't War College classes?

Ironically, the Secretary of the Navy asked the same question in 1888, when he wondered why students weren't finishing the Naval War College faster by taking classes on Saturday and Sunday. This question incensed the founders of the Naval War College, Alfred Thayer Mahan and Stephen B. Luce, who "were livid with anger" according to a history of the College.

> Not only did the Secretary of the Navy fail to understand the education approach of the War College but he threatened its very existence. The college curriculum required large blocks of time for the students to read and to think actively about the abstract problems presented. It was not a course in which data was poured into the ears of students by a series of lectures. The lectures were only a stimulus to the main thrust of the college.[3]

In addition to "how much" education is needed being questioned, and how quickly it can be delivered, "how good" is also apparently fungible. As Chair, I attended a teleconference with other Naval War College leaders where we were instructed by a three-star admiral to "strip out the gold plating" in our curriculum. After it ended, a dumbfounded Navy captain in the group asked: "Were we just told not to excel?" Similarly, in 2011, I was asked to comment on some Navy "cost savings" education proposals and told to keep in mind, "We don't need Ferraris, we need Fords."

At the War College level, calendar "white space" – time left for the students to read and digest the curriculum and for faculty to work on scholarly projects – is viewed as "slack time" and a vulnerability, much like having funds in the budget at the end of a fiscal year. But education, then as now, requires thinking and reflection, which takes time. "Reflection," according to George Reed, "is the essential bridge between experience and learning."[4] Training has right and wrong answers that allow immediate measurement; education is incremental and involves grappling with ambiguity.

The military was once a staunch supporter of the idea that officers needed to be generalists first, broadly educated and comfortable with ambiguity, and specialists later. Many pre-World War II American generals were classically educated, as was the educational tradition of the time. As Secretary of State under President Truman, Army General George Marshall was able to draw analogies between the Peloponnesian War and the post-1945 era. General George Patton's early education included the classics, which would echo in the rousing speeches and battlefield talks for which he would become famous.

Classical education is no longer the norm for military officers though. Technical fields are now favored at the undergraduate and graduate levels of study. One admiral came to the Naval War College and made a strong pitch to the president to change the course toward awarding a Master of Science degree in Military Operations, rather than a Master of Arts degree in National Security Affairs. That would have defeated the whole purpose of the Naval War College and Goldwater-Nichols. Luckily, the proposal was rejected.[5] But technicism and training at all levels still have a fair number of supporters within military leadership.

The differentiation between the goals and methods of education and the goals and methods of training is a distinction that must be continually made to PME administrators and overseers, with differing resultant degrees of success. Discussing the importance of education in raising intelligence analysts' aptitudes, National Intelligence University faculty members Rebecca Frerichs and Stephen DiRienzo state that "education is not an assembly line." They go on to say: "In the simplest terms, training is the process of skills acquisition, while education is the process of knowledge acquisition."[6] Both have value; but they are not the same.

The failure to differentiate between training and education is part of what initially animated the kind of reforms intended by Goldwater-Nichols over two decades ago, and fundamentally reflects, as Wiarda's book title says, a clash of cultures. Cultural issues are always the most difficult to deal with within organizations,[7] especially hybrid organizations, including the military and academic cultures in PME. The same organizational cultural issues that Goldwater-Nichols recognized 20 years ago still persist today. The cultures of both the military and academic faculties are entrenched: neither is bad, nor better than the other, just different.

Differing cultures

The military

Generally speaking, many military officers received their undergraduate degrees in engineering. It is an educational discipline where right and wrong answers prevail: something works, or it doesn't. Admittedly, research and development, and innovation, involves knowing when to break or ignore some of those rules, but knowing and following the rules is the first priority. These officers then went on to successful careers where risk-averse answers to their boss's questions are standard, as are checklists for flying, getting ships underway, and operating nuclear reactors. These individuals are *process* oriented, as following process can keep them alive in high-risk operational situations. Such individuals are well-trained and strong leaders, but neither equates to being broadly educated.

Military officers are constantly being inculcated with leadership skills critical for their operational careers. As part of this inculcation, they are also taught that their leadership skills enable them, with enough training, to do any job. Given the number of combat warriors who have suddenly found themselves planning urban water systems, acting as the unofficial mayor of a village, or building schools and hospitals in Iraq and Afghanistan, the premise is understandable. But pilots, ship drivers, and logisticians can find themselves going from an operational deployment (for which they are exceptionally well trained and competent) one week to being an instructor teaching the Peloponnesian War or how Congress works the next (for which they are often totally unprepared).

Howard Wiarda states that this PME military staffing system is based on the assumption that "every officer is a teacher" merely by virtue of being an officer.[8] They confidently enter their classrooms, though sometimes with little knowledge of the subject they will teach, and are nevertheless often willing to voice strong views on substantive and educational topics. This attitude that "accomplished leaders can do anything" pervades PME institutions where subject matter expertise is often attained by simply declaring oneself to be an expert, and professed based on that self-declaration. (Civilian faculty are just as guilty of this, if not more so, but the basic problem is that the institutions allow it.)

One naval officer, writing for the Naval War College student publication */luce.net/*, considered what happens when hyper-confidence is combined with competitiveness: inflation of achievements. He wrote about his 2010 experience in Basra, Iraq, when a convoy in his unit was struck by a roadside explosive. The gunner was hit with a piece of shrapnel, but fortunately he was not seriously wounded. He was treated, and the mission continued. The author, Commander Jorge Garcia, describes how he was then directed "to write a Meritorious Advancement nomination for the man whose total actions consisted of falling and being a compliant recipient of a bandage to the neck." He states that he wrote a three-page nomination that made the gunner *sound* like an impressive superior performer, though he had actually performed no actions. Garcia says:

> Such deliberate writing (and thinking) is pervasive – and often demanded – throughout the Navy…I do not mean that we routinely lie. Lying has been recognized to be unethical for millennia and is habitually avoided as a crime scene marked with red tape. The malady in question lacks such a universally recognizable face…In a tiny book I picked up four years ago, titled *On Bullshit*, philosopher professor Harry Frankfurt of Princeton argues that "bullshit" is distinct from – and ethically murkier than – lying. In contrast with a liar who holds truth dear as the very thing withheld, a bullshitter's goal is to dazzle his audience with the size and sound

of his statements; their truth is inconsequential. Too many Navy fitness reports and award nominations are characterized this way – they say nothing, impressively... But here is the present state of affairs: Recognition and promotion are concerned with the use (not the truth) of standard phrases, and the presence (not the content) of key documents. This (compounded possibly by a weak liberal arts education) has led to an environment where the phenomenon described by Professor Frankfurt has become a way of life. We naval leaders have become professional bullshitters.[9]

The situation Commander Garcia describes is not limited to operational assignments and situations, but bleeds into statements about achievements and credentials generally. As an NWC department chair, I once provided the faculty with a matrix of dozens of regional and issue-related areas of expertise and asked them to indicate their primary and secondary fields. One retired military officer indicated a primary expertise in almost every category (including regional studies, which would have meant language capabilities, and a depth of knowledge in history, culture, politics, etc.), and seemed annoyed at my audacity in asking. That would seem to qualify as meeting Commander Garcia's definition.

Given the high-pressure, high-stake world that military officers face in their operational jobs, self-assuredness becomes a second-nature survival mechanism, and follows them into non-operational jobs. In fairness, what Commander Garcia calls "bullshitting" is not a trait exclusive to the Navy, or even the military; Malcolm Gladwell calls it being "cocksure." In a July 2009 article in *The New Yorker*, Gladwell talks about what he calls "the psychology of overconfidence" common among achievement-driven individuals, drawing similarities between the decision-making behind the 1915 British-led invasion of Gallipoli and the catastrophic decisions of Wall Street investment bankers in 2008. Gladwell explains:

As novices, we don't trust our judgment. Then we have some success, and begin to feel a little surer of ourselves. Finally, we get to the top of our game and succumb to the trap of thinking that there's nothing we can't master... The British were overconfident at Gallipoli not because Gallipoli didn't matter but, paradoxically, because it did; it was a high-stakes contest, of daunting complexity, and it is often in those circumstances that overconfidence takes root.[10]

A March 2012 article in *Stars and Stripes*[11] asked whether Navy commanding officers (COs) suffer from a by-product of success called the "Bathsheba Syndrome," a term was coined in a 1993 business journal article.[12] The co-author of the original 1993 article, Dean Ludwig, is cited as saying: "Any time someone is promoted into a leadership position, it can engender a sense of privilege, a sense of power and ability to 'cover my tracks.'" The question was raised by *Stars and Stripes* in conjunction with the Navy sacking more than 150 COs for misconduct in the past ten years. The 1993 article is included in the Naval War College ethics curriculum.

While not exclusive to the military, the military also seems particularly willing to accept "add-water-and-stir" experts. Historian Manan Ahmed's article "Flying Blind: U.S. Foreign Policy's Lack of Expertise"[13] discusses the propensity of Americans to equate even minimal personal experience with professional expertise, especially as regional specialists.

Such an "expert" is usually one who has not studied the region, and especially not in any academic capacity. As a result, they do not possess any significant knowledge of its languages, histories or cultures. They are often vetted by the market, having produced a bestselling book or secured a job as a journalist with a major newspaper.[14]

He cites General Stanley McChrystal and Admiral Mike Mullen's stating that they used aid-worker Greg Mortenson's book, *Three Cups of Tea*, as a guide to their civilian strategy in Pakistan as an example. He also describes how technical knowledge is equated to human expertise. While the Air Force says it can "see everything" in Afghanistan with its satellite-based observation technology "Gorgon State", that does not mean that they will be able to interpret accurately what they see. Substituting minimal personal experience for expertise is too often the case in PME.

But, with their qualifications assumed, military faculty quickly acclimatise to faculty life. Daily productivity equates to being in the office for meetings, communal class preparation, and *constant* availability for student consultations. Getting to the office early (first is even better) is a badge of dedication. These individuals are accustomed to 16-hour days on operational duty where they are constantly putting out fires in their areas of specialization. This need to be on operational stand-by carries over. They lean toward a training-like model, using daily critiques, models that explain everything and nothing, right and wrong answers, metrics, and a requirement to learn a limited amount of material only once. They are diligent in their focus to get the students through the program. The world of military officers is, however, completely different from the cultural milieu of their academic colleagues.

Academics

Academics are broadly trained in their fields, although they also spend years developing specializations.[15] Their careers are designed to investigate open-ended questions that often do not have clear answers. (In fact, they question everything, to the point that, sometimes, little gets done beyond raising questions.) They tend to build their reputations and complete their works through individual efforts, working alone. While not always effective communicators in the classroom, almost all of them believe that the best educators have broad intellectual curiosity and should have the breadth to teach beyond that day's PowerPoint slides. Within PME, the academic faculty advocate a broader, open-ended, cumulative educational model.

Academic indicators of productivity cover a wide range of activities: meeting with students during arranged hours, individual class preparation, maintaining an active research agenda, curriculum development and preparation of new lectures, conference presentations, publication commitments, and an open expectation of peer critique. These are not necessarily accomplished between designated "duty hours"[16] or in offices often shared with colleagues, and using information technology so security-laden that it blocks a fair number of their emails and resource venues. Reading a book can be part of an academic's work life, though it probably does not seem like work to their military counterparts. Nobody sees, however, that working on a book manuscript all hours of the day and night for sometimes years is also part of academic life. Academics plan their work in yearly, or longer, blocks, and are *product-* (rather than *process-*) oriented.

Academics are sometimes seen by their military counterparts as self-absorbed, egotistical, elitist, and lazy – and some are. Academics are often elitists regarding academic pedigrees and always read the resumés of other academics with an eye toward "What have you done lately?" All schools, including the War Colleges, have their dead-wood "has beens" and "never-weres." As in civilian universities, longevity for weaker PME faculty is based on popularity with the students, mimicking team-player congeniality, and taking on administrative responsibilities, rather than scholarly activity or teaching rigor.

Without question, as well, academia is burdened with cultural and procedural issues. Most issues, however, are taken up by tenured faculty to an administration forced to deal with them, often in no-holds-barred verbal knife-fights that can leave a lot of bruised feelings and animosity. But issues get aired, and largely settled. All stereotypes are rooted in some truth, and so it is with expressions that describe academics: "herding cats," "fighting over pencils," and "leave academics in a room long enough and they'll vote themselves out of a job" come to mind. Academics are not usually professionally "efficient", individually or collectively. It is not unheard of to hire a former military member into an administrative position at a civilian academic institution to bring some order to chaos – but in very limited numbers and on a selective basis.

There are, unquestionably, civilian academic faculty who come to the War Colleges and are simply more suited to a civilian academic department elsewhere. They are often narrow in their interests with a theory or quantitative focus. They are part of a current debate in academia regarding the "relevance" of political science. Academics Stephen Walt and Lawrence Mead have both recently written about the "gap" between ivory tower and the policy community. Walt provides an explanation for the skepticism about relevance.[17]

> [T]here is a widespread sense that academic research on global affairs is of declining practical value, either as a guide to policymakers or as part of broader public discourse about world affairs. Former policymakers complain that academic writing is "either irrelevant or inaccessible to policymakers...locked within the circle of esoteric scholarly discussion." This tendency helps explain Alexander George's recollection that policymakers' eyes "would glaze as soon as I used the word theory."[18] As Lawrence

Mead noted in 2010: "Today's political scientists often address very narrow questions and they are often preoccupied with method and past literature. Scholars are focusing more on themselves, less on the real world... Research questions are getting smaller and data-gathering is contracting. Inquiry is becoming obscurantist and ingrown.[19]

Beyond issues regarding relevance, not all academics are effective in the classroom. Sometimes they are simply better researchers than teachers. Part of the problem is that, sometimes, universities don't seem to care whether or not faculty are good, or even outstanding teachers, as they give more weight to research in important tenure decisions.[20] An external review once characterized the Duke University history department as "a department in crisis," largely related to a faculty reward system that prioritized research over teaching.[21] Since all professions focus on what they are rewarded for, this makes research a priority for some academics. Neither an institutional model that focusses only on teaching nor only on research is healthy: one leads to cosseting the students, and faculty unable to develop current curriculum; the other leads to treating the students as inconveniences, and faculty not interested in developing curriculum.

Academic faculty who come to PME with a narrow focus and unwilling to broaden their horizons beyond theory or data-crunching, or who prioritize research over teaching, will become frustrated. More importantly, they will frustrate their students as they have little to offer to military professionals. They belong elsewhere and will leave – by their choice or that of the institution, and rightly so.

Mixing oil and water

Within PME, these cultural difference play out in terms of work habits, definitions of productivity, and views on what constitutes education. Military officers and professors have good reasons to be the way they are, but they are not the same. The two cultures are rewarded for doing exact opposite things: academics who do not raise questions are considered poor academics, just as military officers who can't provide answers to their bosses problems don't get promoted. One focusses on product, the other on process. In the War Colleges this plays out as conflict that pits encouraging intellectual curiosity and challenging received wisdom – the very essence of academic inquiry – against the need to prepare graduates for their next assignment.

There is also a natural political clash of cultures that is rarely spoken of, but exists nonetheless. Academics are almost invariably the product of liberal institutions and therefore tend to be liberal, while military officers tend to be conservative – the empirical evidence on that is indisputable.[22] Both cultures tend to be insular and spend considerable time talking to people much like themselves. Whereas Harvard was once characterized by the *Wall Street Journal* as having a "largely left-wing faculty that has about as much intellectual diversity as the Pyongyang parliament"[23] virtually the same can be said for the military, but on the other end of the spectrum.

At the Air War College, for example, a retired Army officer gave what some considered a too-liberal lecture (on the need for the military to be apolitical, as I recall), evident because, at the end, the then-Deputy Commandant stood outside the auditorium yelling "Get that f***ing liberal out of my building!" to the speaker's hapless escort, in full view of the students and faculty. Everybody got the message. Likewise, when curricular materials are questioned by administrators due to "inappropriate" language or deprecating remarks about the military that the students might find offensive (concerns about Max Brooks' *World War Z* comes to mind as an example), there is a chilling effect on education.

Decision-making models differ as well. Though academics certainly defer to, and pander to, their seniors, collegial decision-making seeks and includes input from all. Most civilian faculty departments resolve issues by a vote. That is largely unheard of in PME institutions; I tried it on occasion while a department chair and many military faculty were uncomfortable with the very idea.

In PME, hierarchy prevails. While faculty input into decision-making is sometimes sought, faculty (even military) often perceive that solicitation is perfunctory. Consequently, many faculty keep quiet as they see little chance of effecting change anyway. With the combination of active-duty military and retired military (coming from a hierarchical culture) dominating meetings, a sizeable majority of faculty never come out of "receive mode" in faculty meetings.

Openness and critique does create a dilemma for military commands, which traditionally value – demand – a happy "command climate." Retired admiral and former congressman Joe Sestak reportedly lost his last job in the Navy over negative "command climate" issues.[24] Commands are supposed to reflect teamwork functioning at its best – key in an operational environment where people can die from mistakes.[25] Part of the problem, however, is that operational commands, especially combat commands, often bear little resemblance to PME academic campuses. Nevertheless, administrators at all commands have vested interests in perpetuating the image that all is well.

A happy command climate and one that encourages dissent and critical discussion are not necessarily mutually exclusive. In fact, there is a Navy expression, "A bitching sailor is a happy sailor... only start worrying when they stop complaining!" That, however, is not the approach supported in PME. It has been the case throughout my PME career, attending at least one "all hands" faculty meetings per year, that rarely are *any* questions asked or comments made when the Admiral or General opens the meeting for discussion, and that silence seems perfectly acceptable to administrators.

While each new commander is required to take a command climate survey (of employees, so at PME institutions students are not included), there is no requirement for transparency or specificity regarding the results. The survey information is for the command's informational use. Hence there are attempts to downplay or outright bury issues ranging from those like sexual harassment to hostile work environment and questionable hiring and violations of ethical boundaries, lest they reflect poorly on the command.

I was once told, for example, that gender-related "hostile work environment" issues I knew had been raised on the command climate survey (by other faculty) were not being pursued because they were not statistically significant. That was technically true, but only because the number of women was, and is, so low – at least partly because of a perceived hostile work environment – that it resulted in a(nother) Catch-22: even if every one of them reported a hostile work environment, they would be only a small fraction of the result, and so they are statistically insignificant: QED.[26] So when there is good news it is shouted from the rooftops; but when it is not, the survey results simply disappear or are presented to the faculty and staff as three or four bulleted, generic, "concerns we're looking into."

Further, many individuals do not trust the survey's anonymity because it is administered on government computers and demographic information is requested. Since PME institutions are overwhelmingly dominated by white males, anyone not in that category can be easily identified. Hence there is a reluctance to raise sensitive issues that individuals feel will be traced back to them, and they will then be identified as "a problem."

Fear of being tagged "a problem" for raising issues goes beyond command climate surveys. As the senior woman at more than one PME institution I have had many women students and faculty – and a surprising number of men – visit my office in frustration, aghast or angry over issues ranging from comments made by students or instructors in class (including racial slurs about the 44th President of the United States) to personnel policies. I always suggested that these comments be taken up with the administration, but all feared, and some experienced, being tagged "a problem" by virtue of having raised concerns.

To be clear, contract academic faculty are largely cowered from directly raising issues to the administration about anything for fear of it effecting their employment. Students, on the other hand, are more than willing to raise issues to the administration that are the responsibility of the faculty – the curriculum, too much work, schedules, teaching methods, etc. – in fact, they are encouraged to do so by a system that constantly pulses them to ensure that they are happy. But, students know better than to raise issues that are the responsibility of the command. That can get them tagged "a problem". As a former military officer explained: "It is, after all, not real world but only academic play, so why anger or alienate a senior over it?"

When issues raised anonymously on command climate surveys are pursued, both the methods and intent for doing so can be ambiguous. As a department chair, I was once called in and told that multiple negative comments had been raised about my department and my leadership team on the latest command climate survey, and I was required to respond to them, which I was eager to do. Uniformly, however, they were so generic as to be meaningless without context. They focussed on, for example, not "being team players." I asked whether the issues were raised internally or externally, so that I could direct my answer appropriately. Anonymity required that information could not be revealed. Was each comment raised by a different individual, or multiple comments by one person? Two or three persons? Again, that information was considered confidential. Were the comments directed at me personally, someone else, or the department as a group? That information could not be provided.

Nevertheless, I fully addressed each of the six issue areas delivered to me, providing both the president and provost with a response binder of over 100 pages, covering multiple interpretations of the generic complaints, and including 23 tabs of support documentation. I subsequently also twice requested an appointment with the president to discuss what I considered the likely underlying issues motivating the comments, and my counters. That request was eventually turned down with a cheerful email from him saying: "You have taken the required actions and, frankly, I consider the issue closed…Thanks again for your report, it was very helpful to me."

Who manages the mix?

While the rhetoric of top military leaders supports education for strategic leadership, the actions of those below them often favor technical disciplines and training methods, or simply not being willing to allow top performers to take time from operational assignments for education without career penalty. This initial mismatch between rhetoric and action is then exacerbated by placing PME execution in the hands of risk-averse administrators largely inexperienced in the field of education generally or academic administration specifically. They are also responsible for assuring a productive hybrid military–academic cultural mix, but rarely have either the background, experience, or penchant to do so.

PME administrators are not just content with the status quo – a training model – but promote it because to do otherwise would take them into areas beyond their competencies and, consequently, could, theoretically, jeopardize their jobs. The importance of this administrative situation cannot be overstated. Nobody thinks that experience as an academic department chair would deem someone to be qualified to command a helicopter squadron. If such an individual were to somehow land in such a position, though, their instinct might well be to have the helicopters leave the ground no more than absolutely necessary, rely on those who will minimize risk and thereby maximize success rates even if defined solely by "no accidents" rather than safely achieving mission goals, and hide their lack of knowledge as much as possible, if only by bluster. Bringing in pilots, ship drivers and others with little or no experience in academia and putting them in charge of educational missions bears much the same results.

Having more broadly trained academics with experience in higher education as PME administrators would promote – though not guarantee – the use of best practices based on experience toward a more rigorous and effective program. Currently, PME frequently replicates the worst dysfunctions found in the most mediocre civilian institution, combines that with a process-oriented training model, and calls it education. Too often I have heard administrators claim "they called a friend"(always anonymous) in academia to check on academic practices; one provost often overruled the academic department chairs in educational policy matters, relying heavily, we were told, on the advice of his brother in the computer industry. This just doesn't work.

There are multiple issues that stem from the core issues of the military services favoring training over education and inexperienced, career-focussed non-academic administrators. But development of an academic program geared more toward development of students' intellectual agility, rather than training, will be dependent on fixing these issues first. There is, however, a complicating issue. Specifically, there is an inherent tension between academic standards that would favor such agility, and the services' investment in their professional officer corps, which makes it imperative that all students be successful at the War Colleges. Therefore, a closer look at the student body is in order.

3 The students
Too valuable to fail

The final reason the military is ill-suited to breeding creativity among its leaders is the military bureaucracy itself. Bureaucracies, by their very nature, reward conformity above all else.[1] Take the typical military career path. From commissioning, most officers have a fairly good idea what they need to do to make O-6, the general benchmark of a successful military career. Hard work. Yes. Some level of competency. Sure. But assuming the talent and drive is there, nowhere along that path does it require one to take risks, question how things are done, and certainly not question why they're done. Those traits might actually derail one's path to O-6. Conformity is rewarded with silver eagles.

Commander John P. Buser, USN[2]

All PME learning, like most adult education programs, centers around seminar groups. These seminars of 13–15 students represent the Army, Navy, Air Force and Marines, plus perhaps civilians from a U.S. government agency, most likely the State Department or an intelligence organization. Each seminar also includes international officers, especially valuable in discussions for their non-American perspective.[a] There is a strict non-attribution policy in the seminars to encourage

---

a International officers attend U.S. War Colleges largely to learn about American culture and ways of thinking, rather than an academic education, with a considerable amount of travel included in their program toward that goal. Their participation in seminar discussions can be very helpful in avoiding American group-think, though their language capabilities can vary. Inclusion in these programs is considered a badge of distinction among many foreign militaries. Some PME schools grade these international officers on their classwork. Doing so, however, opens a host of problems and issues that the Naval War College has wisely avoided by recognizing the program as primarily one of foreign policy rather than academics, and not grading them.

students to express themselves freely – without fear of retribution – toward the aim of advancing critical thinking.

For faculty, whether retired military or practitioners who have spent their careers working on security issues, or academics who focussed on security-related topics through years of graduate school and experience, working with PME students can be one of the strongest motivators behind both hiring and retention. The students bring unique knowledge to seminars that can immensely enrich the discussion. For instance, Latin-American drug war discussions that include individuals who spent tours tasked to find and intercept drug runners bring seminars to life. The difficulties of nation-building are far more relevant when one of the students has been the acting mayor of a village in Iraq, charged not only with security but also responsible for getting the water running and the schools open. Theoretical topics like nationalism become tangible when a helicopter pilot suggests that, if shot down in Iraq and you can see two villages – one awash with flags and the other one with no flags evident – it is safer to go to the village without flags as those villagers are less likely to be nationalistic zealots. There are moments of stunning insight in the classrooms, largely unmatched in civilian institutions.

War College students are mid-career professionals with children and elderly parents. Many come from high-pressure jobs, intense operational experience, and very competitive environments. They are not college students. Many, however, don't like to read, coming from an oral tradition of commands and briefings, and it has likely been years since they have written anything other than bullets on a report or a PowerPoint slide; and again, many have degrees in engineering. It takes them a significant amount of time to transition from their previous assignment to being a student, and some never make the transition.

I have had PME students who were among the best I have ever taught in any institution. One went on to be an aide to a four-star general whom, I am confident, he served well. Another served two tours in Iraq and then went on to get a doctorate. I wrote a letter of recommendation in support of his doctoral program application. I stated that not only was he among the top students I had ever had the privilege to teach, but also that if my son were in the military I would want this individual to be his commanding officer as he is one of the finest individuals and leaders I have ever met. I am confident that both of these individuals could hold their own and contribute to any graduate program in the country and, more importantly, in national strategic debates. Unfortunately, the former officer retired soon after his aide tour, feeling his strategic talents would not serve him well in career advancement. The latter was required to get his doctorate in engineering, rather than a social science, and was told that his chances of career advancement would be affected, and not positively, by making the decision to pursue an advanced degree. These students are exemplary, and many faculty connect with and stay connected with these types.

Some students recognize the value of their PME opportunity immediately and fully embrace it. For others, it takes longer. While I was Chair, faculty in my department regularly received communications from former students, either offering testimonials to what they had learned and perhaps not then appreciated, or requesting curricular materials to "reread," finding it directly related to their current assignment.

In the classroom, however, many PME students are average or even mediocre classroom performers, having little to offer in discussions not directly related to their career experiences, and doing mediocre work on assignments. Some students do not hold back voicing their view that a course is "irrelevant academic BS" on day one of classes – before discussion even begins – and often thereafter.[b] Some seminars are lively and engaged; others are largely quiet and passive. Many students like to stay in the comfort zone of what they are good at, and often that doesn't include some or all aspects of a liberal arts graduate education, most of all writing. Writing is not what they do, or want to do. But it is what they need to do.

Admiral James Stavridis, NATO's Supreme Allied Commander Europe, has encouraged students to leave their comfort zones and write an analytic essay.

> The enormous irony of the military profession is that we are huge risk takers in what we do operationally – flying airplanes on and off a carrier, driving a ship through a sea state five typhoon, walking point with your platoon in southern Afghanistan – but publishing an article, posting a blog, or speaking to the media can scare us badly. We are happy to take personal risk or operational risk, but too many of us won't take career risk.[3]

b   That specific term was conveyed by a colleague, though I and others have had similar experiences as well.

Despite non-attribution policies, student aversion to career-risk issues manifest and project in different ways, depending in part on whether the students want to be a War College resident student and the process through which they arrived.

Avoiding risk is a two-way street in PME. Students do not want to leave their comfort zones, fearing failure, and PME institutions have a vested interest in the success of their students not found in civilian institutions. Failing a student in a civilian graduate program means that a (usually) young adult must recover quickly or redirect his/her career plans; failing in a PME program could mean the end of a career for a highly trained and valuable member of the military – valuable both in terms of their ability to contribute to the military mission and in terms of investment made in the individual with taxpayer money. Dan Hughes states:

> A student who fails to graduate probably would not be promoted, would not be qualified for joint assignments, and would become a retiree in a relatively short period of time. Since the services invest at least $300,000 per student per year, to say nothing of the incalculable investment made in every officer prior to service school attendance, the reluctance to cause or even recognize failure is understandable in some quarters.[4]

While the basis for the $300,000 figure is not provided, the overall point of service investment in the officers is valid.

According to a former Assistant Dean of Students at the Naval War College, there is usually a small handful of students who for health or family reasons are not able to complete the course within the standard ten-month period. They are simply recycled through when able. There may also be one or two students who do not graduate because of academic violations, such as plagiarism. That may mean not being awarded a Master's degree, and occur only in the most egregious cases (and are usually civilians, whose careers are considered more expendable).

No one wants to harm an officer's career over an academic issue, so in most cases of academic integrity violations individuals are allowed a "do over." Failing a course, and therefore failing to graduate for poor performance, is virtually unheard of, and the students know that.[5] As posted on Tom Ricks' blog, *Best Defense*, in April 2012: "Overheard the other day in reference to the rigor at PME: 'It's hard to get an A; it's even harder to get a C.'"[6] In a system where a normal admissions process, with consideration given to past academic records and merit capability as determined by standardized tests (usually the Graduate Record Exam) is non-existent, nevertheless virtually everyone graduates in ten months.

Student admissions and matriculation

Goldwater-Nichols mandated that all military officers complete Joint Profession Military Education (JPME) in two stages during the course of their careers, either in residence at PME institutions or through associated distance programs. The courses are called Joint Professional Military Education, Phase 1 (or the Intermediate Level Course, ILC) taught at Command and Staff Colleges, and Joint Professional Military Education, Phase 2 (or the Senior Level Course, SLC), taught at War Colleges. It is important to note that each of the Army, Navy, and Air Force War Colleges have both a resident and a non-resident program, necessary to fulfill the Goldwater-Nichols mandate of education for all officers. The resident programs simply cannot handle the volume, nor are the military services willing to give up the manpower and time for all officers to take a ten-month resident course. Whereas, according to their websites, the resident SLC student body at the Naval War College was 242 in 2011–12, there were over 5,000 students enrolled in NWC distance education programs;[7] and, similarly, 250 resident students at the Air War College and over 5000 in distance programs.[8]

War College programs began awarding accredited graduate degrees in the 1980s.[9] The decision to award a Master's degree was the result of several factors, including the congressional intent to wed academic rigor to military education, the need to signal the purpose of the colleges, and student demand that a year of study merited a degree. On a practical level, the War Colleges found that students were determined to get a degree one way or another, often enrolling in night programs at local colleges or universities: Salve Regina in Newport, University of Alabama, Montgomery near the Air War College, and Shippensburg University or Penn State Harrisburg in Pennsylvania all saw a fair share of degree-seeking night students from the military over the years. Since there was (and still is) little chance of failure at the War Colleges, the students naturally focussed most of their attention on satisfying the degree requirements at the civilian schools in order to gain the degree that they correctly thought was going to be more useful over the long term (read, after retirement) than a sure-thing JPME box-check requirement.

Each service has a different attitude toward education, and consequently a different process for deciding who they send to the War College resident programs. In general, officers from all of the services except the Navy competitively apply to attend War Colleges in residence, and there may be a second round of competitive application if an individual wants to attend a service school affiliated with a branch of the military other than their own. For these individuals, promotion is tacitly or explicitly linked to academic achievement, though certainly not outweighed by operational experience. Navy students, until recently, and still depending on their respective warfare community (aviation, submariner, surface warfare officer, etc.), often shared – in a non-attribution environment – that they were cautioned by both detailers and superior officers that War College attendance could actually hurt their career since it takes time when they could have been deployed and working with senior mentors.[10] Navy fitness reports on which promotions are based do not indicate whether JPME was completed in residence or through distance options; it's the same box to be checked either way.

Air Force selection for resident War College attendance is done in tandem with selection for promotion to colonel and lieutenant colonel. Those at the top of the promotion list then get first priority to apply to the War College of their choice, with the default placement being the Air War College. These students, for the most part, are slated for further assignments after completion of their PME experience, and represent the cream of the operational crop, though that does not inherently mean that those selected possess the greatest potential for critical and strategic thinking.

Army and Marine students similarly apply for acceptance to the resident programs. For these students as well, a second application process determines which students will go to the school of their choice, rather than their own service school by default. When students are required to apply competitively for admission, they generally tend to be better students. They are also, however, focussed on grades – which has both positive and negative impact on their expectations and performance. Everyone graduates, but for the non-Navy students, graduating at the top of the class gets favorable consideration by promotion boards.

Navy students are assigned into War College billets (positions) on a non-competitive basis. While some Navy students are top performers, others are admittedly placed in NWC billets under a "put a body in a seat" selection basis. For many years, the Navy operational communities were underrepresented, while the medical community, lawyers, logisticians, supply officers and other staff jobs were overrepresented within PME student bodies. In recent years, however, there has been a more balanced representation of the naval communities.

Now, however, another situation takes top Navy students from the classroom in Newport. A number of special groups (designated as the Halsey Group, and the Stockdale Group, for example) have been created to research and respond to topical Navy issues and are populated with top students. The problems created are twofold. First, the students have had no education on how to conduct such research; and second, it takes these individuals out of the seminar mix where "learning from each other" is supposedly key.

For those students who tend toward doing the minimum, that attitude is exacerbated by senior officers who, over the years, have repeatedly reminded students from the Naval War College auditorium stage that "it's only a lot of reading if you do it," or referred to the auditoriums of both Maxwell and Newport as "the big blue bedrooms." To say that general disdain for education, especially non-technical education, among some superiors affects student choices and attitudes would be an understatement. Students attending the Air War College at Maxwell joke that it is a year to improve their golf handicap. Remember, all will graduate, and many students are not looking for or expecting a next promotion once they reach the War College level.

Former Army War College faculty member Wayne Silkett experienced similar lax student attitudes at the Army War College:

At the [Army War College] after a grueling Wednesday morning spent vainly trying to stay on the subject at hand (it was a nice day with tee times at stake and Wednesday afternoons were off for students – ostensibly for research and reflection) I gave up in frustration and walked out of the seminar room. A few minutes later one of my students stopped by my office to say, "Hey, Wayne, don't take it so seriously. We don't."[11]

Rarely is War College attendance characterized as a year of rigorous study.

Students attending War Colleges are frequently told by their personnel officers and superiors that it will be a year to reconnect with families and relax. This presents a real dilemma. Officers, Army and Marine officers especially, have been sent to the War Colleges from a tour, or tours, in war zones. They are legitimately expecting time to reconnect with their families before potentially being deployed again, often into command positions. While that does not inherently negate the premise of academic rigor, it does influence War College leadership who see their mission as graduating students, rather than educating students for the next level of their careers, and providing a program that is comfortable and doable for potentially weary officers.

The wars in Iraq and Afghanistan have seriously constricted time available in an officer's career for study. The former commandant of the Army War College, General (ret) Robert Scales, lamented the apparent deterioration of the value placed on PME in a 2010 article:

> Throughout the services officers are avoiding attendance in schools, and school lengths are being shortened. The Army's full-term staff college is now attended by fewer and fewer officers. The best and the brightest are avoiding the War Colleges in favor of service in Iraq and Afghanistan. The average age of War College students has increased from 41 to 45, making this institution a preparation for retirement rather than a launching platform for strategic leadership.[12]

The result, Scales argues, is that War Colleges are now "intellectual backwaters;" more "preparation for retirement", he says, than "a launching platform for strategic leadership." The fact that a War College may be an officer's last assignment before retirement certainly casts doubt on how much anyone ever cared about the "return on investment" in an officer's career. The former commandant's frustration is palpable, and understandable to anyone who has ever taught in PME.

With the wars placing increased demands on officers' time, the services have become creative in how to fulfill their congressionally mandated JPME educational obligations to send both students and faculty to War Colleges. It is not unusual for active-duty military to be a faculty member in one War College department and simultaneously a student in another, earning the same JPME credit and Master's degree as their students. At least at the Naval War College, that officer may well be deemed enough of an expert in the curricular material taught in one of the three departments to begin immediately teaching alongside others who have studied the materials over the course of a career, and to also be a student in the other two departments during other parts of the year. After sometimes little more than two years, that officer then leaves with a Master's degree, and their service has fulfilled its obligation to send both a military faculty member and student to a tour at the War College.

Further, once the services decide who they will send to a War College, the colleges themselves have little say regarding acceptance. Rarely is a student deemed an unacceptable candidate. For a time the Navy was trying to send increasingly younger and more just-before-retirement students to the Naval War College, and the College successfully pushed back. But the kind of rigorous admissions process that is the norm for quality Master's programs, the caliber of which the War Colleges like to consider themselves the peer, simply does not exist.

Consequently, the War College educational experience is often, for better or worse, only what the students make of it. To be sure, there are some who are dedicated students, who work hard, and grow intellectually in their time in residence. Students who were unlikely candidates for graduate study in the first place, or were dragooned to attend, will pass with good grades alongside their more exceptional colleagues, with little distinction in their final records. Some, however, adhere to the unofficial but oft-quoted maxim of students at the Naval Academy: "if the minimum weren't good enough, it wouldn't be the minimum."

Student attitudes

My colleague Tom Nichols tells a story relevant to understanding student attitudes at the War Colleges. Renowned physicist Robert Jastrow taught at Dartmouth College in the 1980s and gave a talk about missile defense to a student audience. A proponent of missile defense, Jastrow got into an increasingly technical back-and-forth discourse with an undergraduate student on the topic. Realizing that he was no match for Jastrow, the student sought to end the exchange without conceding defeat by saying, "Okay, we'll just have to disagree. Your guess is as good as mine." To that Jastrow returned a simple, but blistering retort: "No, no, my guesses are much, *much* better than yours."

War College students are told throughout their careers that their opinions, on pretty much everything, are as good as everybody else's – except their superior officers. But, unlike Jastrow, contract academic faculty at War Colleges are not in a position to tell a student they don't know what they are talking about, as student evaluations can mean the difference between an extended contract or being out of a job. Military faculty, on the other hand, often nurture the idea that all opinions are valid, either as a mentoring device for the younger versions of themselves, or because they are not subject matter experts themselves. In any case, too often War College students graduate with the same wrong, misguided, or narrow views with which they entered.

David Maxwell suggested in his 2012 *Small Wars Journal* article that "in order to increase the intellectual capacity of the services it may be time to consider education separate from rank and conventional timelines."[13] While the intellectual arguments in support of that approach make sense, cultural impediments would persist. Military officers are inherently rank-conscious; they sometimes do not take kindly to having those junior to them, in terms of either age or experience, challenge their views or grade them. Sometimes, as well, experiential gaps within seminars (seminars where some officers have been in command or held staff positions while others are more junior) legitimize their complaints – something I often heard as a department chair – that seminar discussions are most useful among peers. Other times, complaints are simply based on who outranks whom. In an end-of-course group exercise, Naval War College students were allowed to pick their own leader within their seminar, rather than having that position held automatically by the senior officer in the group. When one of my seminars dared to select a dynamic young officer rather than the senior curmudgeon who had hampered seminar discussions throughout the course, the senior officer not only complained to me that he was *entitled* to lead the group, but also then sulked and did not participate usefully.

Uniforms designate rank, and junior officers often defer to senior officers in what are intended as academic discussions. At the National War College, the Naval War College, and the Army War College, students do not wear uniforms unless told to for a special event, and so designated a "uniform day," in part to try to level the playing-field in classroom discussions. At the Air War College, students wear uniforms to class. For a while, one commandant even designated Friday as "warrior day" at the Air War College. (A similar effort was defeated at the Naval War College.) On those days students would wear their fatigues and flight suits to class. Even in civilian clothes there can be a tendency for junior officers to defer to senior officers in class discussions. In uniform, that tendency is even more pronounced.

In a seminar discussion at the Air War College, I noticed students getting uncomfortable as I talked about satellite images showing the ozone hole getting bigger, and the issues it created. I finally asked the very dominant senior seminar leader if there was a problem. He replied decisively that, in fact, there was, as I was inferring a flaw in God's plan with talk of an ozone hole. Dumbstruck, I turned to another student, a (lower-ranking) dermatologist, and asked if his community felt that a thinning ozone layer increased the risk of skin cancer. Looking toward the senior officer he said he had heard of no such link.

While students are encouraged by (some) faculty to think "outside the box"[14] while at the War Colleges, they are often concerned about who will read their work and whether there will be professional "blowback." A student from the submariner community, for example, once asked me if the papers would be made available externally as he wanted to write a paper supporting the use of diesel submarines and feared superiors in his field – the nuclear Navy – would read it and subsequently tag him as "not a team player." Based on the experience of a junior Air Force officer, his concern was justified.

A February 2009 publication of Air University called *The Wright Stuff* included a controversial article questioning the value of ICBMs, written by Air Force Major Mike Faunda while he was a student at Air University.[15] Soon thereafter, Faunda found himself the target of a brutal rebuke in the same publication, co-authored by three lieutenant colonels and supported (by name) by 15 others, all commanders of missile squadrons.[16] While academic freedom encourages debate, the berating given to Major Faunda by superiors in his career field will not be lost on other junior officers, who will likely be reluctant to similarly "think outside the box", publicly, in the future.

An interesting quote from a midshipman posted at the Naval Academy's English department website demonstrates that acculturation toward rules, and consequently risk aversion, begins early in the military. The quote says simply: "English lets you think outside the box and not get in trouble for it."[17] Similarly, a quote from educator John Dewey in 1899 (mistakenly, or perhaps jokingly, attributed to Mao) was tacked to the wall by an anonymous wag at the Naval War College: "The children who know how to think for themselves spoil the harmony of the collective society that is coming, where everyone would be interdependent."

Another impediment to education rather than training in the classroom is that few military students have significant interest in any topic or subject not immediately related to their next *individual* assignment, albeit for good reason – they're trained *not* to. They are trained to stay focussed. War College curricula must be relevant to security practitioners at large, and prepare military officers to keep up with the best and brightest of their civilian peers in future assignments. But students too often expect classes to be directly relevant to their next job. If they feel that their schoolwork is not going to help them directly in the next 18 months, they do not hold back on their complaints to the administration, even though they cannot possibly fully know what will be "relevant" given the length of their careers.

Finally, although they may be brave leaders and professionals in their operational jobs, when officers come to PME they take on characteristics of college students in general. Individuals who once worked interminably long days at the Pentagon, or who even came under fire in the field, suddenly find it unbearable to take two exams in a week or to write an eight-page paper. Like their often much younger counterparts in undergraduate and graduate programs, they want (and often expect) faculty members to provide them with copies of their classroom teaching slides – problematic for reasons ranging from attribution issues to the prospect of deliberately controversial or provocative comments placed on slides for the purpose of generating classroom discussion potentially being taken out of context elsewhere. Slides can be the equivalent of personal teaching notes. The especially perplexing part is that students seek these even in classes where grades rest solely on analytical papers rather than testing of particular material, and so are of little value in relation to grades. But time becomes precious and expectations rise, especially for those for whom academic performance is even remotely linked to promotion. Grades, as at the best civilian universities, inflate while the tolerance for work shrinks.

As a department chair, I regularly held meetings with student representatives, where students often asked questions whose answers were easily found in the comprehensive syllabus with which they had been provided but which they had obviously not bothered to read. Students generally do not read instructions given to them because they assume their instructors will tell them anything really important. This assumption is even higher among military students used to verbal commands. There were many interesting requests and complaints. Students who work hours in operational jobs beginning before the sun comes up complained about occasionally having to be in class at 0800 rather than 0830. Imperfect copies of readings provided free to them were brought to my attention as unacceptable, though printed elsewhere. Having a paper due the same week as an exam generated complaints, though the due date and exam date had been announced at the beginning of the term so that students could plan accordingly. Some students wanted more lectures, some wanted fewer. In many ways, PME students are like students everywhere; whatever half of them want, the other half wants exactly the opposite, and rarely are any of them satisfied completely.

In terms of expectations of the faculty, however, PME students surpass others. Perhaps most telling, a student once complained to me that he could not appropriately fill out the requested end-of-course evaluation of the course and faculty until after he had his grade, because if he didn't get an A, *it was clearly the fault of the professor!* As unthinkable as it would sound in civilian academia, it was not until well into my tenure as Chair that I was able to do away with a system where students actually did receive their grades before they evaluated their professors, and instead implemented the standard double-blind system of professors issuing grades prior to seeing their evaluations and students evaluating courses and faculty before seeing their grades.

My initial response to these kinds of student requests and complaints was to ask the group at large if they represented consensus views, and most students were (rightly) embarrassed and said they were not. Nevertheless, individuals were not hesitant to raise each and every one of their complaints and perceived slights by the faculty on their exit survey. These surveys were read with Talmudic scrutiny and Illuminati-like secrecy by the administration, followed by proclamations about "student views" – loosely translated as "what they like" – to which the faculty was expected to respond.

The institutional dilemma

PME institutions suffer from a problem that also plagues their civilian counterparts: they care too much about what the students like and want. In fact, the propensity to care about what the students like is worse in PME schools, because PME is organized around the notion that the students and faculty are *peers* – an idea no academic institution anywhere else would take seriously. Both the faculty and the students are professionals in their own fields, and should be respected as such, but they are not peers. Even worse, when I first arrived at the Naval War College, the students were referred to by the military faculty as "clients" or "customers", a practice it took me years to end.

PME students can provide valuable insight and input into the learning process. But just as doctors and lawyers are both professionals, a lawyer does not tell a surgeon how to operate, and a surgeon does not defend himself in a malpractice suit. Doctors and lawyers are not professional peers, just as PME faculty and students are not peers; if they were, why would faculty be needed at all?

The idea that students are peers creates a confusing, if not outright difficult, environment. For example, one way the team-building aspect of the military culture plays out in PME is a tradition of having faculty members – like a wing commander or the skipper of a ship – have a party at their home for the students and their spouses (sometimes children too) at the beginning of the course. I've seen these range from cocktail parties to potluck dinners to hootenannies with guitars and banjos to full-blown sit-down dinner parties with extravagant meals and plenty of alcohol. Ironically, an increasing number of students with busy schedules, young children, and working spouses, do not really care for this 1960s-like military socializing as much as some of the retired military faculty do.

The academic faculty, especially the junior faculty, often object, either because they don't have a housing situation and budget to support this kind of entertaining, or because they prefer to keep a professional distance from students who are often older than them. This "keeping a professional distance between teacher and student" approach has its advocates. Georgetown University professor and Jesuit priest, Father James Schall states:

Knowing students too well can in fact be something of an impediment to learning, especially for the other students in the class. The activity of learning goes on, perhaps even better, when student and teacher are addressing themselves to the matter at hand, to the reason why they are in the same place, at the same time, with a kind of mutual awe before something they neither created nor made.[18]

His further point that "the essential 'activity' of teaching and learning is mostly independent of the personal relationship of student and teacher,"[19] can be broadly applied. Some teachers and students will become friends; it should not, however, be an expectation for classroom success.

The idea that students are peers also creates murky personal dynamics. An Army lawyer told me that at the Army War College there is a clear, written prohibition against faculty–student personal relationships. At the Air War College, I attended the wedding of a female faculty member and a male student. Both were active-duty. The faculty member had never had the student in class, and they were of the same rank. In Newport, while faculty–student relationships are prohibited, what is not clear is whether that means in all instances or between faculty and students whom they will grade. A male civilian faculty member faced an investigation and suspension without pay after he met a female military student (not in his seminar) at a bar in town, and she gave him her phone number, but then later complained to the NWC administration about sexual harassment. What are the rules regarding personal relationships if faculty and students are considered equals?

Howard Wiarda noted in his memoir of the National War College that he had taught at many schools but had never seen one so focussed on the whims of such "pampered" students as National, and he found it "laughable" that he was required to consider them as equals. The issue, he points out, was not whether the students had input to offer, but the inordinate fear among the administrators that the graduates would one day punish the institution if their egos were bruised in any way:

Everything seemed to depend on whether the *students* were happy and satisfied. The reason for this, I was told by one of the deans, is that it's the students who, if unhappy for any reasons, complain to the Joint Chiefs. The faculty cannot do that... [or] the student will wait until they become generals and admirals...and mete out their revenge then. [One commandant] waited fifteen years to wreak his revenge on National for some real or perceived faults.[20]

Wiarda bitterly referred to this constant placing of students "on a pedestal" above their teachers as a "chicken-hearted policy" that produced nothing good. While his criticism is scorching, Wiarda has a point about students' attitudes and the effect on education.

Student grades is the area where institutional attitudes toward the students – they *must* succeed – are perhaps most clearly evident. Since everyone graduates, there is a significant difference between policy and reality. The Naval War College Student Handbook, for example, states official policy:

> Grades provide the faculty a means of determining the degree to which course materials have been absorbed and understood, and provide direct feedback to the students. Grades assigned by faculty for papers, exams, class participation, etc., are expressed as letter grades and their numeric equivalents. All the work in the Electives Program will be graded on a High Pass/Pass/Fail scale. The core curriculum courses are graded using the standards indicated in each syllabus.
>
> Historically, normal grade distribution has been 35–45% As and 55–66% Bs and Cs. Students must attain a grade of "C" or better in all prescribed courses as well as passing grades in the elective in order to fulfill the academic requirements for graduation. A grade of B– or better in each of the prescribed courses must be attained to fulfill requirements for the Master of Arts degree in National Security and Strategic Studies.

So, officially, students can get a grade lower than a B–, and can academically fail to graduate and/or receive a Master's degree.

In 2003, at the Naval War College, however, the president asked the then Strategy & Policy Department chairman if anyone had ever failed the course. After researching the answer with the registrar, it was found that the last recorded academic failure had occurred in 1998 when one student received a C. The next most recent instance was in 1994, when a student received a C+ for the course. Those were the only academic failures on record. According to the departmental executive assistant (an active-duty Navy captain) who researched the question for the chairman, he also obtained some anecdotal information on the subject of substandard academic performance from the former chairman of the department, who was still in residence. The former chairman recalled one or two instances, paraphrased in a memo to the then chairman. The department was informed in each instance that there had been "exceptional circumstances," such as personal or family issues, and that the department's recommendation of failure was overridden by the president of the Naval War College in furtherance of United States Navy interests.

In 20 years of teaching in PME I have never given anything below a B– as a final course grade, nor am I personally aware of anyone who has. The average grade for students in my department while I was chair was consistently around 89.5%. For other departments it was often higher. While faculty are often told, and I told my faculty, to give the students the grade they deserve, the reality is that faculty know the institution wants the students to graduate. While officially we do not grade on a curve, we do in reality, with grades ranging largely from 84–95.

Dan Hughes reports similar issues regarding grading practices Air War College, with institutional norms dictating grades as much as, or more than, merit. His explanation is worth quoting at length, as it is true in PME generally.

> By and large, there are no real academic standards, a fact to which new professors quietly object but which they, like the older hands, eventually accept with resignation tempered with dark humor... In 2009, the war fighting department gave the grade of "A" or "A–" to more than 97% of the students in its core course... For academic year 2010, the dean reinstated an old "goal" of no more than 50% "A" and "A–" grades. A professor who assigns low grades or too much work in an elective endangers future enrollment, thus jeopardizing continued employment...
>
> For decades, the Air War College has appended one element to its academic program that is largely unknown to academic graduate institutions: remediation of course failures. Students who failed examinations (which rarely happens) or who produced unacceptable papers traditionally had the absolute right to re-accomplish that task because the officers are viewed as expensive assets that

cannot be allowed to fail. Virtually 100 percent of those who fail the first time pass the second effort.

Professors are reluctant to give grades of "C" or less because the remediation process punishes them rather than failing the students. In fact, the professors frequently consult with each other to determine if anything is to be gained by forcing a student to repeat an assignment. If the student lacks the ability to improve his performance, there is no reason to force him or her to do it over since the end result is the same as giving a meaningless "B" or "B–" the first time.[21]

Hughes' point is clear. The military has invested a significant amount of time and money in an officer's career, making them the military equivalent of "too big to fail."[22]

If PME institutions decided to grade students based strictly on individual performance, the services would probably have something to say about that. Scott Bethel, Aaron Prupas, Tomislav Ruby, and Michael Smith discuss the problem in conjunction with developing Air Force strategists:

> Many of the papers submitted for awards or publication are heavily edited by faculty to ensure that they are cogent and worthy products; the students simply do not know how to conduct critical analysis. Indeed, there is no lack of passion in the papers, but there is a great void where evidence and reason should be. When some Air University leaders argue for grading according to the objectively earned grades of all students, others respond that the Air Force Chief of Staff would never stand for a large number of his top-tier majors barely passing the course.[23]

This inherent tension between academic standards and the service's investment in their professional officer corps is *not of the students' making*. They are the *beneficiaries* of that tension, not the *creators* of it. Consequently, however, students at the War Colleges, far more than in civilian institutions, wield too much power over contract-dependent faculty and insecure administrators, to the detriment of the educational mission and, ultimately, PME's actual clients – DOD senior leaders and commanders and the American people.

So, while students' input is crucial and must be valued to improve

PME curriculum, it should be solicited judiciously; they should not dictate the educational goals and methods of PME (or any academic institution). However, because PME faculty are uniquely beholden to their students "liking" them to the point of deference, there is little internal impetus for change from the faculty. The administration has become a bureaucracy, dedicated to self-perpetuation, growth of administrative jobs, and graduating students. The circle is closed.

4 Faculty

But not necessarily in a collegial sense

In a completely rational society, the best of us would be teachers and the rest of us would have to settle for something else.

Lee Iacocca

Any college is only as good as its faculty. The basic differences between faculty at civilian colleges and in PME are the hiring process and faculty involvement in governance. Faculty at civilian academic institutions are largely hired based on some merit criteria (which admittedly differs among institutions) and curricular need, with the goal of keeping their best performers. At the War Colleges, a significant portion of the faculty is assigned to them by the military services, with little regard to teaching or academic ability, or even interest, and another portion is hired, retained, or fired, too often based on criteria other than academic merit. Faculty in civilian institutions are part of the governance system; in PME they are kept out. What emerges is a case study on how, if the core body of active academic professionals is excluded from governance and major policy decisions, a training rather than educational model easily comes to prevail.

Faculty are those usually identified as individuals holding academic rank at an academic institution. *College* has many definitions, including a building used for educational purposes, and an organized body of persons engaged in a common pursuit or having common interests or duties. While certainly War Colleges are buildings used for educational purposes, whether the college is an organized body of persons in pursuit of common interests is a different question. Whereas a college faculty is normally fully engaged in institutional governance – where the common interests and duties come to play – in War Colleges faculty have little or no role in institutional governance. In fact, they are deliberately kept out.

The role and expectations of faculty

At civilian academic institutions, faculty play key roles in who is hired as their peers, and their administrators, and regularly voice their opinions to the administration through sometimes powerful faculty senates. Academic rank separates junior faculty from senior faculty, with progression from assistant to associate professor a required professional rite of passage. Further, junior faculty clearly understand that many college professors will never reach the most senior rank of full professor, reserved for a prominent and especially productive few. Within the military, when someone reaches the rank of colonel or captain, their peers know that that individual has achieved that status through very high professional achievements, including command responsibilities. Similarly, in academia, when someone reaches the rank of full professor, their peers expect that very high professional achievements have been met as well, within the areas of teaching, research and professional service.

The tenure system means that junior faculty are initially on probation, having to prove themselves to their internal and external professional peers, the senior faculty, and the administration. Once tenured, however, they are assured of a career position (unless dismissed for cause), allowing them to speak freely in their subject areas of expertise and faculty governance matters without fear of retribution. The idea is that those who can speak freely will do so for the good of their chosen profession (most civilian academic salaries being what they are, it's not for the money) and the educational goals of the institution. Academic politics can certainly be petty and vicious. Henry Kissinger once quipped, "University politics are so vicious precisely because the stakes are so small."[1] But they are for the most part open and transparent – or at least personnel rules are known and the administration held to them.

The best and the brightest civilian academic faculty will rarely consider coming to an institution that cannot assure three things: (1) academic freedom, (2) a comprehensible career path, and (3) time to pursue the individual research that marks the standing of academic professionals in their field. The Naval War College has been a leader on the first point, as its presidents and the Navy itself have defended the long tradition of academic freedom – witness this book – and original research. Other PME institutions have been less fortunate in this regard, thus less able to establish their own academic identity.

The latter two points, however, are shaky ground for all the War Colleges, for a variety of reasons. As a hybrid institution – a military command with an educational purpose – the faculty role in governance, key in considerations of rank and hiring, is minimized or manipulated to be virtually non-existent. Time to pursue professional activities can be considered unnecessary, or a waste of time/money, because most of the military faculty and administration have no professional interests they want to pursue. Most of all, though, War College faculties are rarely tenured, making it impossible to voice opinions freely without fear (real or not) of reprisals. Therefore, whether they are working toward a common educational purpose, rather than individually focussed on keeping their jobs, becomes a serious issue.

Every competent profession, academic or otherwise, requires a career path that is transparent and merit-based, but neither of these are a given in PME institutions. I joined the Air War College as a senior associate professor (the same rank I had held in the Florida university system), and subsequently applied for promotion to full professor. This baffled the administration. As I later found out, no one knew how to promote academics to a higher rank because I was the first faculty member *not* to be hired as a full professor, regardless of prior rank or academic qualifications. (I was also the only civilian woman then on the faculty, which may or may not have been a coincidence.) Although I was promoted, the why and how were largely undisclosed.

The Naval War College also lacked promotion procedures. Everyone was hired as a full professor, regardless of qualifications, until the early 2000s. That included not just retired military officers, but a 30-year-old Ph.D. of less than three years, which would have been unheard of outside PME. To rectify this situation, which hurt the credibility of the institution and made hiring difficult, in 2004 my colleagues and I put forward a proposal for a merit-based career path.

The proposal was met with fierce resistance, indeed outright fury, by military retirees who felt that almost any military service justified the most senior academic title regardless of other qualifications (or lack thereof). This reaction not only emphasized how devalued the title of "professor" had become at the War Colleges – not least because it was viewed as an entitlement, not an achievement – but the ensuing debate revealed how little thought was being given to what it means to be an "educator" or even "to educate." The retirees who spoke out felt entitled to be hired as full professors *solely* based on their past military rank, and bristled at the notion that they should have to do anything further to develop themselves as faculty once on board.

In fact, one military retiree in a key administrative position at the Naval War College openly admitted that he rejected the proposal for merit-based ranks because few if any of his faculty would be able to compete for any academic rank under such a system. Worse, he countered with a proposal that "the president [of the War College] establish a policy whereby all future Deans, Department Chairmen and Directors have a minimum of 20 years' career military service," which would exclude all civilian academics (and, as we pointed out, several secretaries of defense and presidents of the United States) from any leadership position and thus end further challenges to the status quo. While (a revised version of) the initial proposal for a rank system was accepted, and the counterproposal rejected, the proportion of retirees in senior positions remains, nonetheless, quite high, and those ranks continue to grow.

Some War Colleges at times have offered tenure, or tenure equivalents, through something called "indefinite contracts," meaning that they do not have to be renewed after a particular number of years, with an expectation that the individual will serve until retirement. The Naval War College offers indefinite contracts on a limited basis and, until recently, a very secretive basis. For many years, those who held these contracts were believed by the faculty to number seven,[2] so they were referred to as "The Magnificent Seven." Faculty quietly speculated on who held them, and how they were granted, with the general feeling that they were largely granted by the president as a reward for service; a former active-duty dean of academics who later joined the faculty as a civilian faculty member was, for example, known to hold an indefinite contract. In one case, though, a scholar of note was also granted an indefinite contract after he was shortlisted for a faculty position at a prestigious college, with tenure. Finally, in 2004, when the academic rank policy was put forward, a policy was also written to allow faculty to apply for these coveted contracts based on merit, and at least one faculty member has been granted one under the new policy guidelines.

In 2008, I similarly applied for an indefinite contract under the policy in place. The provost, a retired officer, subsequently decided a new committee was needed to reconsider the policy process and the 2004 guidelines. Though the committee met several times, it was unable to reach any conclusions. The meetings were largely non-productive, with three competing arguments put forward.

First, the retired military faculty argued that there was no need for these contracts, but if they were to be more widely distributed, they deserved them most of all. Second, academics who had abandoned their professional academic careers argued that contracts without term should be granted for service rendered, meaning longevity. Third, academics with active professional careers supported the idea that contracts without term should be granted to those in supervisory roles, to young talent seen as particularly important to the future of the institution, and in the cases of particular faculty merit.

During the long committee process it was learned that two more faculty had been granted these contracts since 2004, but quietly. Finally, months later as the president was preparing to retire, still without a new policy in place, he issued an email communication to all faculty and staff thanking the committee for its work, which remained unfinished. He then went on to say that I had met the criteria of the policy, awarded me a contract without term, and publicly announced for the first time the names of others who held them. Whether any have been issued since is unknown. The committee never met again to discuss policy criteria.

The Air War College, for its part, offered tenure while I was there, and then stopped. Dan Hughes explained the ensuing situation:

> Beginning in 1990, the Air University instituted a tenure system similar to those at most universities, but then abolished it after 2000. Instead, it offers initial appointments of three years and subsequent renewals of periods from one to five years. Those persons who had tenure were allowed to keep it, but those hired into tenure-track positions were given a gruesome choice. Air University schools offered renewals longer than a single year only to professors who agreed to give up their tenure-track appointment. Since a single-year renewal suggested termination at the end of that period, every untenured professor eventually chose the longer appointment.[3]

These erratic and seemingly arbitrary personnel policy changes can be unsettling, to say the least, to civilian academics.

Faculty at all of the War Colleges have similar stories of erratic hiring, rank, and retention. At National War College, for example, Howard Wiarda was told point-blank that there would never be a tenure system of any kind because it would interfere with the commandant's ability, in effect, to do as he pleased with the faculty, who were all considered interchangeable, and many of whom he wished to frighten, intimidate, or fire to make way for friends he wished to hire.[4]

At an April 2012 panel discussion on Professional Military Education in Washington, D.C., Major General Robert Scales – a distinguished officer and genuine American war hero – adamantly proclaimed that student evaluations were not used in civilian faculty contract renewal decisions when he was commandant at the Army War College. He even called on an Army War College faculty member in the audience who had worked for him, and is still on the faculty, to support that contention. The faculty member respectfully demurred, noting that as a senior faculty member he frequently had colleagues come to his office for counsel, concerned that their contracts would not be renewed for reasons ranging from student evaluations to having been seen wearing an "Obama for President" button. Scales then went further, claiming to have not been aware that student evaluations were even taken at Carlisle, an odd assertion given that they are required as part of both JPME and accreditation for the Master's degree at all War Colleges. General Scales also steadfastly rejected the notion of faculty tenure, in favor of allowing the leadership "flexibility" in staffing. He maintained that position even when it was pointed out that military officers effectively have tenure in that after a set number of years of proving themselves they are told – just like civilians in the academic world, or partners in a law firm – that they may expect a career of 20 years or more until retirement, unless dismissed for cause. Further, the military, unlike civilian faculty under a contract system, are not faced with potentially being summarily fired in middle age – without cause and often with no appeal – and their pension still far in the future.[5]

Theoretically, how well any faculty member has achieved the goals of the institution, and therefore how likely they are to be invited to stay on, should be reflected in their annual evaluations, which is one reason why these are required. This should not be difficult or mysterious, but faculty trust in the system is undermined when "trapdoors" are built into their contracts, such as fuzzy requirements to "demonstrate commitment to jointness," "capture efficiencies," or "challenge assumptions" – all inserted into Newport's faculty contracts for a period. (How such a disempowered and timid faculty were supposed to challenge *anything*, much less DOD's assumptions, was never explained.)

More recently in Newport, administrative focus has been on standardizing the annual faculty evaluation process. Theoretically, this is aimed at evaluating and rewarding faculty on the same criteria across the entire college – which would be a good thing. As a practical matter, however, such a goal is impossible. Because some of the language has been created by bureaucrats and administrators who do not have an academic background, the categories in which academics are traditionally evaluated – teaching, research and service – have been redefined in ways that no academic institution would recognize. "Curriculum" and "scholarship", for example, are divided, despite the fact that they are closely related, and dependent upon each other; "professional activities" (which other schools would simply call "service to the profession") have been reorganized so that routine in-house tasks are evaluated on the same level as major external professional activities. Ostensibly, the object is to standardize evaluations; the real impact is more opportunity for administrators to justify negative evaluations and hence exercise power over the faculty.

All of this assumes, too, that a faculty member actually receives an evaluation. I once did not receive a written evaluation for six consecutive years, despite my repeated written and verbal requests, although my performance must have been satisfactory during this period as I was annually rewarded with bonuses, albeit without further explanation or feedback.

To its credit, the Naval War College, more than any other non-tenure-granting PME institution, adheres fairly closely to an academic tenure system, where faculty are, essentially, permanent after six years of service (though many faculty are reluctant to trust that, for obvious reasons). Some fail to reach that mark, but they at least have some protections from arbitrary decisions after that six-year mark, including the right to appeal. Faculty at other PME institutions, however, report that they can be, and have been, fired at will after years, even decades, as faculty by capricious administrators and senior officers hiding behind opaque processes, with no explanation and no recourse.

Administrators often try to keep faculty off-balance and timid by hints – and sometimes blatant scare tactics – about budget cuts threatening jobs. Phrases like "institutional changing budget numbers" and "a storm is coming" are used in conjunction with allusion being made to lists of faculty being drawn up potentially to be fired. Frequently, however, these veiled threats occur at the same time that new flat-screen televisions are being installed throughout the college buildings, iPads passed out,[a] and new faculty are being hired to perform jobs that nobody can adequately describe, including more administrators. The administrators always seem to fend off the impending budget doom, but for new faculty these budget-scare campaigns can be intimidating:

Some officers are open about not wanting civilian academic faculty of any kind at the War Colleges. Major General Robert Scales has argued for replacing all faculty at War Colleges with active-duty officers:

> Virtually all attempts to reform professional military education have failed principally because these efforts have been driven by academics who focus reform on curricula and faculty hiring. The truth is, PME reform is not a pedagogical problem. It's a personnel problem that can be addressed only by changing the military's reward system to favor those with the intellectual right stuff... The insidious creep of the civilian contractor must be reversed such that virtually all ROTC, service academy, and staff and War College faculty positions be filled by uniformed officers. Those positions at service PME institutions better suited to civilian instructors should be filled with long service professionals from government agencies such as State, Agency for International Development, Commerce, Homeland Security, or the Office of Management and Budget, as well as a liberal infusion of professional staffers from congressional committees.

Both the spirit of Goldwater-Nichols and the qualitative and quantitative limitations of military faculty, however, challenge the viability of General Scale's solution.

George Reed challenges the viability of General Scales solution as well:

> I must disagree with General Scales on the desirability of repopulating the system of professional military education with uniformed

---

a Admittedly, there are different categories of government money, some of which can be exclusively used for one thing but not another.

officers at the senior service college level unless they have both a credible professional and academic background, and that means more than a single tour on the faculty at an undergraduate service academy. I too would like to see the services value teaching in the system of professional military education as he suggests, but military officers who comprise much of the faculty, at least at the Air and Army War Colleges, simply do not have enough time on station to really get good at teaching.[6]

The entire issue of diversity within faculty composition inherently keeps returning to the underlying question of education versus training. If education is the goal, as Goldwater-Nichols demands, then civilians must be included in the faculty mix and every attempt should be made to get and retain the best teachers and scholars.

Part of hiring and retaining top civilian faculty is creating work schedules that allow time for accomplishment of actual scholarship and its associated products. This means recognizing that faculty need blocks of time for scholarly work that is not constantly sacrificed to the erratic "taskings" and time-consuming, unproductive office routines that are more appropriate to a low-level bureaucrat than a top teacher and researcher – the kind of work senior military officers unload to junior officers. Faculty understand rank and hierarchy, but they are not junior officers or intellectual valets.

As George Reed states:

> Having served in both systems I also have to say that professors in the system of professional military education just aren't treated as well in comparison to those in the civil sphere. In terms of pay and benefits, discretionary time, developmental opportunities, support for research, the ability to consult, and the license to pursue one's own agenda, civilian academe wins over the War College hands down.[7]

I have to disagree somewhat, as the faculty teaching load at PME institutions can be significantly lighter than at some civilian institutions, especially for junior faculty, and the pay scale higher. Further, each institution is different, but at least at the Naval War College significant strides have been achieved over the past several years toward allowing faculty the kind of time and opportunity for the professional development Reed refers to. But each step forward has been hard fought and remains tenuous, with many faculty reluctant to trust that policies won't change again.

For example, whether faculty should be writing articles and books, under what circumstances, and whether the government owns the copyright, has been almost a constant topic and changed policy throughout my career at three institutions. Guidelines varied significantly between institutions as well, based on what the administration wanted and what the resident legal officer interpreted the relevant regulations to mean at a particular point in time.

My Naval War College colleagues and I argued for reasonable publishing guidelines that differentiated between work tasked to individuals and developed for the government – and therefore government work product with the government owning the copyright – and work undertaken as part of their professional development, where the copyright would be owned by the individual.[8] The "rules" for government work products seemed set; the guidelines for other work were ambiguous, and often under scrutiny with more administration control and approvals being considered necessary.

Discussion about the appropriateness of, and guidelines for, writing books, in particular, stopped at the Naval War College after a faculty member, and Pentagon favorite, wrote a *New York Times* best-selling book.[9] According to the author, in the preface of the book, the book was derived from a PowerPoint brief he had developed as a government employee and given "a hundred times to several thousand Defense Department officials."[10] The sale of the book was then promoted across the country, all with NWC institutional approval according to the author[11] (and from the perspective of many NWC faculty). Faculty questions regarding whether this meant the rules regarding writing books from government work products had changed and was acceptable went unaddressed. The author was taken to task, however, after students began complaining about his book being hawked from the NWC stage. The author resigned from the Naval War College[12] to write a second book, and almost immediately had an interview with Secretary of Defense Donald Rumsfeld, which was published in *Esquire*,[13] evidencing (at least to the faculty) that if there was censure, it was limited at best.

The reasonable guidelines previously argued have since become tacit policy. In fact, in his last "President's Forum" written from the

Naval War College, former president, Admiral Phil Wisecup, touted the "books and articles that faculty or, in some cases, students were publishing."[14]

The larger issue of the "appropriateness" of scholarly activity as part of faculty responsibilities extends even further. Not only do the "rules" for scholarly writing vary among PME institutions, but they also can vary depending on institutional leadership, including the military lawyer in residence at any given time. One NWC legal officer once suggested putting "counters" on faculty computers and requiring faculty to keep track of time spent working on projects directly benefiting the Navy and those for scholarly or professional development. The idea was to push the latter to be done largely during "non duty" hours at home. The department chairs countered by asking if faculty would be paid overtime for the considerable grading, reading, and preparation for class they did at home; the startled answer being "no."

The general idea that academics inherently do not work a set schedule is anathema to the military. Further, the administration has included a requirement for faculty to maintain their professional expertise in their contracts; and as faculty note, they cannot then hinder or block them from doing so as part of their daily work. The counter idea was dropped, but policies often change when administrators change, and faculty are constantly on the lookout for the next bad idea with which they will have to contend.

Clearly some PME institutions understand the importance of not just allowing but also supporting faculty in their contractual requirement to stay current in their fields. Army General H.R. McMaster thanks West Point in the acknowledgements of his 1997 book *Dereliction of Duty*,[15] written while he was a faculty member in the history department there. More recently, Naval Postgraduate School faculty member James Clay Moltz says, in the acknowledgements in his 2012 book *Asia's Space Race*: "This book would not have been possible without support from the Naval Postgraduate School's Office of Sponsored Research, which provided me with two academic quarters of research and travel funding through the Research Initiation Program."[16]

Faculty largely understand that in writing and speaking they have academic freedom to speak for themselves, but not for the institution. On articles, for example, including a disclaimer is common policy and practice – something like: "The views expressed in this article are the author's alone and do not represent the official position of the

Department of the Navy, the Department of Defense, or the U.S. government." While publishers don't always include them, most faculty are acutely aware of the need to include them in written works and in talks. With War College websites increasingly publicizing faculty publications and activities, recognition of the positive aspects of faculty work seems gradually recognized by the services and the Department of Defense.

Nevertheless, the sometimes rigid structure and arbitrariness of PME often means the brightest stars, if they can be convinced to join the faculty, will soon leave for more intellectually and professionally rewarding careers. Having some of the best and brightest leave for other positions is understandable, and even desirable, if the War Colleges benefit from the "halo effect" of being seen as a desirable place to launch a career. If, however, faculty are running from what is considered an intolerable place to work, that too will become known and will affect negatively faculty recruiting.

Many of those who stay do so out of inertia, for the relatively high salaries, or for lack of other opportunities. It is a truism that many academics do not "come" to PME but, rather, "end up" there. The War Colleges have indeed made some outstanding hires by capitalizing on the brutally tight academic job market, and from occasional mistakes of university tenure committees.

Dr. Janeen Klinger, then at Marine Corps University, addressed the issue of recruitment in a 2004 article, "Academics and Professional Military Education," where she argued on behalf of broadening the background of civilian academics recruited to PME, and discussed the difficulties of doing so. She specifically says, "the discipline that has been overlooked is anthropology."[17] As a department chair, I recommended hiring an anthropologist to the Naval War College faculty. He was hired but did not stay very long. He never seemed to adjust to the military culture of the organization. The more diversified the disciplines of civilian academics brought into PME, the more difficult it becomes to suppress or deny a military–academic culture clash.

Whereas for some academics the need to be generalists at War Colleges is difficult, because academics study for years to become specialists, for others the breadth of a War College curriculum can be attractive. Civilian academic departments can be stifling in their requirements that faculty members focus on theoretically "expanding the discipline" in ways that may or may not interest an individual over a career of decades. The best War College faculty, however, will be specialists in their own fields (which is often geared more to the policy arena than to academic theory) and generalists able to teach a broad curriculum as well. The requirement to be a generalist stems from War College curricula developed collectively, and everyone within a department or subcourse (some departments subdivide large amounts of curricular material into more manageable parts) teaching basically the same material.

Still, the easy, training-style goals found in PME can have a great attraction for civilian academics whose careers never took off (or sputtered out quickly), since predictable and repetitive teaching tasks relieve them of facing any new challenges. The institutions not only allow, but also in many instances actually support such an attitude toward leveling the playing field between military, retired military, and civilian faculty. Thomas Bruscino, an assistant professor at the U.S. Army School of Advanced Military Studies, explains the dumbing down of academic knowledge so that all faculty can teach it:

> The military's concern, quite frankly, is with the application of academic knowledge to their craft. If an academic cannot explain why a subject matters in the most practical of terms, that subject appears to have no real value. Real expertise, and the less obvious benefits of such expertise, can too often get lost in translation. When academics introduce some of the contentious but highly specialized debates from their respective field into this environment, they are often accused of arguing over how many angels can dance on the head of a pin, or, less charitably, for contemplating the fuzz in their navels. Lest they be accused of too much naval gazing, hundreds of academics in the military's employ leave behind their professional standards and spend most of their time doing work that they know any reasonably bright master's student could handle.[18]

Such faculty respond to the bureaucratic norms of the military institution and do only what is required to gain their next contract renewal, rather than remaining engaged with their external peers and adhering to the greater standards of the profession: worse, some simply invent or inflate accomplishments. Unfortunately, it is not unusual for individuals to be appointed to endowed chairs or center directorships in areas in which they have no substantive background, and suddenly be deemed experts in those fields; international relations theorists or historians suddenly become terrorism experts or economists. This damages both the credibility of the institution and other faculty members.

But PME faculty *must* be active in the disciplines where their ideas are debated, and refined, so that they can offer the best curriculum to their students, who are charged with preventing and planning for war. Quick trips to war zones to get "street cred," as an increasing number of PME faculty are doing, cannot replace serious scholarship on issues of peace and war. Though argued to "strengthen the curriculum" and "validate classroom concepts"[19] the experience gained has a short shelf-life for educational purposes.

Moreover, there is a difference between year-long deployments where individuals have specific jobs, and individuals dropping into busy commands for short periods. Some by-name-requested individuals or those with specific expertise undoubtedly serve valuable purposes, even if for short periods; but, according to a War College faculty member who served a full-year tour in Afghanistan, his command turned away volunteers who would only come for 90 days as they had little to contribute and lacked the commitment to see plans through to execution. "During war," he said, "there is no time for military tourism." Those departments most lacking in professional scholarship, or attempting to substitute "street cred" for professional scholarship, will inherently be the ones with the most moribund curriculum.

Similarly, as well, while country visits can enhance one's knowledge of a country or region, quick trips alone do not establish anyone as a regional expert. Regional experts will have extended knowledge of the culture, history, and language of the region. Expertise takes time to establish in any field and must be tested against, and by, peers.

A quick perusal of resumés on the web from the faculties of any of the War Colleges reveals both very impressive careers, in fields ranging from U.S. history to nuclear strategy and American presidential politics, and others less so. One long-serving civilian faculty member states on his institutional website that he is working on a "big book," apparently a *magnum opus*, which explains why his last book was published during the Carter administration. Another proudly states that he is the author of "several" books, though no titles are provided, and an internet search reveals no evidence of these several books. Faculty members feel the need to embellish their records to establish credibility with the students, and the largely non-academic administrators.

Those who have stopped being productive scholars are often competent teachers, but cannot mentor younger faculty or help develop the institution itself. Much like the adjuncts on contract mills in lesser civilian schools they can come to see themselves as contractors rather than as faculty, and thus default to an occupational model of academia where teaching is a job, rather than a profession.[20]

Faculty workloads differ between institutions, and even between departments within institutions. A 2011 chart produced by the Center for Strategic and Budgetary Analysis indicated what the military services pay in terms of "cost per student" at the various War Colleges, with the Naval War College cost ($57,000) less than half that of either the Army ($166,000) or the Air (about $120,000) War Colleges.[21] Cost savings at the Naval War College are largely attributable to two factors: Newport students do not take often extremely expensive regional studies trips to other countries as part of the curriculum, as do students at the National[22] and Air War Colleges,[23] and even more importantly, one faculty teaches for the Navy what two separate faculties teach for the Army and Air Force. For the Navy, both the ILC and the SLC courses are taught in Newport by the same faculty during different trimesters, with that same faculty also responsible for developing the curriculum for both. The Army and Air Force have two buildings and two faculties, one each for the ILC and SLC.

Within departments, workload requirements differ also. Publishing is sometimes a requirement as a demonstration of professional engagement with external peers, though often not in departments largely populated by retired military. Those who do not publish might teach electives more frequently, in a niche subject they can develop once and then repeat annually. Often, faculty who are not active in the scholarly fields will purport that they do not have time to do so, because their focus is on the curriculum. The irony is that without active scholarly engagement, they do not have the substantive ability or knowledge necessary to create curriculum.

Curriculum development needs vary by department. Those who teach historical material have less curriculum development requirements – the outcomes of the Peloponnesian War and the Battle of Leyte Gulf do not change from year to year – than those teaching policy-related material. How much curricular material must be covered in particular departments is dictated per joint staff guidance, so some departments have more student contact hours than others. All of this is supposed to be balanced out on an individual basis with department chairs, but quite naturally some individuals often feel that they bear more of a burden than others.

Most War Colleges have faculty handbooks that state academic, workload, and personnel policies. For the most part, the handbooks focus on processes and standards to be upheld regarding academic freedom, workloads, hiring, and promotion, all subject to interpretation by the Dean of the Faculty, Dean of Academics, or Provost, depending on the institution. Subsequently, handbook policies become fungible. Exceptions can and are made regularly to all guidelines, except when the guidelines serve administrative purposes.

Dan Hughes points out that – regardless of what is written down – War Colleges are institutions run by the rule of men, not of laws. He explains the system at the Air War College:

> The College's rules and procedural guidelines, called "operating instructions" (OI; now with new names, but basically the same items), govern most major activities in extraordinary detail and seem to be a mechanism for creating a very orderly organization. In practice, though, an OI has value and provides guidelines only when management wishes to use it to enforce its desires. When that is not the case, management changes the suddenly obsolete OI, frequently without even informing the faculty and sometimes retroactively. OIs thus govern labor but not management. This is, once again, entirely in accordance with the needs of a military organization and produces only a harmless cynicism among some professors. The colonels seem quite accustomed to the arbitrary exercise of authority from on high, and the professors soon come to accept it or leave. It is a sign of their loyalty to the institution that they do not routinely warn job candidates of this issue during the hiring process.[24]

Frank discussions in candidate interviews often leads to losing candidates. The composition of the faculty and the administration is key to understanding institutional dynamics, warranting a close look.

Military faculty

Although PME faculties are composed of civilian and military members, it is often difficult even to define or differentiate between those categories as a careful look at the "civilian" faculty roster in PME faculty positions would reveal that many are actually retired military officers.[25] This is because military officers can retire while still quite young, immediately draw a full pension, and go right back to work, many on the government payroll. This questionable and expensive practice was targeted for overhaul by former Secretary of Defense Robert Gates, and left on the table by his successor Leon Panetta.[26] Similar practices are not available to other government employees, such as those from the State Department who must, in effect, choose between their full pension and a full-time government position.

While the effects of this retirement policy are far-reaching across the Department of Defense, the result in PME is that many active duty military members assigned to War Colleges as their twilight tour (just prior to retirement) make the circular argument that they are qualified to spend their retirement teaching at a War College because they have already taught at a War College. But military faculty assigned to the War Colleges are often not qualified for the position, nor considered the best and the brightest by the military services. Some military faculty simply get "stashed' at War Colleges because they have been a problem elsewhere.

Dan Hughes explains the situation at the Air War College:

> The Air Force routinely sends colonels who are out of favor to ride out their final years at the Air War College. One had been relieved over the 2007 nuclear warhead incident at Minot Air Force Base. Another had been held responsible for the crash of a very expensive airplane. One was emotionally disturbed, having claimed to have suffered all kinds of abuse while on embassy duty. Others remain on the faculty for many years because no other Air Force agency wants them.[27]

George Reed describes a similar situation at the Army War College:

> A central problem with staffing the War Colleges stems from the fact that the colleges have little control of who the services assign

there as military faculty members. The personnel system seems to believe that any old colonel can do, but examples to the contrary abound. Assignments are made for a host of reasons that do not relate to one's ability or even interest in teaching. I remember one particularly egregious case where the Air Force sent an officer to the Army War College who suffered from a noticeable speech impediment.[28]

The key point is that the services have no control over who is assigned as a military faculty member. For the Army, Air Force, and Marines, which tacitly or explicitly link educational achievement to the promotion process, *it is easier and less competitive to be assigned to a War College as a faculty member than it is as a student.* Students are selected for attendance by a competitive process; not so for the faculty. For the Navy, any day not spent at sea is a wasted day, so assignment to the War College often is not by choice, except perhaps as a twilight tour.

Beyond obvious impediments, there are several other issues related to the teaching competency of military faculty as well. First, unless they are assigned to a War College department responsible for teaching military operations, they rarely arrive as subject matter experts. In the operations department, active-duty military personnel are clearly needed, preferably those with command experience. In the other departments, though, the idea that any pilot or ship driver can teach history, politics, economics, or international relations with little preparation assumes that depth and subject matter expertise are not really needed, even when teaching the subjects at the graduate level.

Second, like their civilian academic counterparts, not all military officers are good teachers. While many might be excellent at imparting training skills, that does not always translate into seminar-style teaching. Reed explains the situation at the Army War College, which is more or less common to all:

We used to quip that you merely survive the first year as a faculty member, begin to become competent at the second, and when you are finally comfortable in the seminar room it is time to go. The experience of military faculty members is respected, and they have instant credibility with the student, but experience and good teaching do not always go hand in hand.[29]

But if these individuals can establish their willingness to be "team players" at the War Colleges, their careers can rise like a Phoenix within the organization, potentially even to include a retirement position, bestowed by their retired colleagues-cum-administrators.

And that is the real issue: non-academic administrators, in practice, sometimes have used their flexible hiring authority to circumvent merit-based hiring in general, and instead hire those loyal to maintaining the status quo, regardless of qualification, including many active-duty military hired directly from their active-duty tour into civilian faculty and staff positions. This is possible because civilian War College faculty, unlike most other government employees, are not part of the General Schedule (GS) civil service system (Title 5 of the U.S. Code), but instead are hired under the ostensibly more flexible Title 10, which has fewer explicit requirements for hiring and firing.

In theory, Title 10 provides the government with the ability to change faculty as needed under various circumstances. This means that faculty work on short-term contracts – anywhere from one to four years, and up to six years at institutions like West Point – and can be refused contract renewal for almost any reason. Title 10 positions are not always advertised or competed for, and people are sometimes hired into a vacancy quickly and their contracts need not be renewed when their services are no longer required.

There is an underlying logic to this. If experts on European integration were hired when the Berlin Wall fell, but those same positions needed to be filled later by counterterrorism specialists after 9/11, there would be the flexibility to make that change. In practice, however, that is not how academics approach their profession, nor how colleges manage their faculties. All professional schools create chairs and programs for topical issues, but they do not consider a faculty member who is not the "flavor of the month" the equivalent of "dead wood." (Academic faculty become "dead wood" when they no longer choose to maintain active engagement with their field, and cease publishing or developing new courses.)

Regarding the hiring of retired military as civilian faculty, again George Reed describes the situation from the perspective of his time at the Army War College:

> Retired officers are a mixed bag. They are often completely dedicated to the institution and bring a lifetime of experience, but

without a deep underlying reservoir of disciplinary knowledge and a strong desire to stay connected and contribute to it, they can get a bit stale. They rarely leave voluntarily and the administration rewards their loyalty, if not their contributions, by renewing their contracts. Their experiences have a shelf life that begins to expire on the date of retirement. They can usually be counted on to run a good seminar, but few contribute much in terms of scholarship as measured by the usual indicators of research and publication... They can be powerfully resistant to change...[30]

Looking ahead to their impending retirement, then, officers will emulate these successful retirees and spend their last military assignment at the War Colleges doing whatever is needed to assure a post at the institution after leaving the service, in general by demonstrating their reliability as guardians of the status quo, and ostracizing uniformed colleagues who advocate change.

When civilian professors complain about the use of differing standards in the hiring and treatment of retired military officers as faculty, they can sometimes find themselves facing charges that they are disruptive, and even suffer retaliation. In 2011, for example, law professor Tim Bakken, a civilian at the U.S. Military Academy at West Point, sued the Department of the Army, claiming he had been discriminated against by the Academy via his department chair, Colonel Maritza Ryan, after he reported discriminatory practices that favored retired military officers, such as giving them time off to obtain advanced degrees, and granting them higher salaries despite their lack of qualifications. After making his claims, Bakken suddenly found his employment record criticized by Academy leaders, despite a decade of praise and excellent evaluations by his superiors. Col. Ryan (who later in court would describe Bakken as "divisive") then rearranged Bakken's teaching schedule to give him heavier duties. She also "told [Bakken] that he should not be a 'negative force' within the faculty and cadets" and that "she did not expect him to be 'sowing the seeds of discord.'"[31] Bakken claimed that all of this was retaliation, and in 2012, a U.S. Federal administrative judge agreed, finding that the criticisms of Bakken's work were "wholly inconsistent" with previous evaluations by the Academy, and that Bakken had suffered "a significant change in [his] working conditions." West Point was subsequently ordered to restore Bakken to his previous duties. Incidents like this might explain why retired officers remain the faculty of choice for military administrators looking for "team players," and why even in tight budgetary times, there seem to be plenty of jobs for those retirees to go around.

Beyond extensive non-resident academic programs, the service colleges have grown in recent years to encompass far more than graduating officers, offering a plethora of job opportunities for retirees. In addition to the intermediate and senior courses taught in Newport, a number of new colleges, centers, and programs have been created as the Naval War College mission has been expanded.[b] At the Naval War College, for example, the Center for Naval Warfare Studies (CNWS) "links NWC to the fleet and Washington policy makers as a source of strategic and operational thought."[32] The College of Operational and Strategic Leadership (COSL) provides "leadership continuum of Professional Military Education for Navy Personnel."[33] The Senior Enlisted Academy (SEA) "provides senior enlisted leaders resident and distance education in communications skills, leadership and management, national security affairs, Navy programs and physical fitness."[34] All these are under the auspices of the Naval War College and all hire "professors" – mainly retired military – making job options plentiful and qualifications flexible. Thus, "rocking the boat" is perilous for military officers wanting to stay after retirement.

Processes and practices that reward loyalty over merit are unfortunate because they obscure the fact that military faculty can, and do, play a vital role at War Colleges. No other group can better calibrate the delicate balance between theory and practical material by bringing operational relevance to the curriculum and maintaining ongoing operational connections to operational commands. And, without doubt,

---

b   The 1994 Naval War College Self-Study, provides a statement of the college mission: "The mission of the Naval War College, as approved by the Chief of Naval Operations on 28 October 1992, is: to enhance the professional capabilities of its students to make sound decisions in command, staff and management positions in naval, joint and combined environments; to provide them with a sound understanding of military strategy and operational art; and to instill in them joint attitudes and perspectives; to serve as a center for research and gaming leading that will develop advanced strategic, warfighting and campaign concepts for the future employment of maritime, joint and combined forces" (p. 1). By the 2009 NWC Self-Study, the mission description is now five paragraphs, one each focussing on: development of strategic and operational leaders; help CNO define the future Navy and its roles and missions; support combat readiness; strengthen maritime security operations; and deliver excellent support (pp. 1–2, 1–3).

while many officers are solid instructors, some are born *teachers*. Some are blossoming scholars as well, able to combine their operational experience and scholarly analysis in important and sometimes unique ways. I have co-authored articles on space with military faculty at both the Air War College and the Naval War College because of their specialized knowledge and to assist in easing them into writing for publication.

Indeed, there are military faculty members, retired and active-duty, who not just hold their own against the civilian academics but also even carve specialized, valuable substantive niches for themselves. Besides being outstanding in seminar, they become subject matter experts in areas ranging from geographical regions (including language capabilities) to fields like defense economics, where few civilian academics have any subject matter expertise. These individuals become and remain professionally active externally through a variety of venues and methods, and can demonstrate professional development annually.

Some military faculty, however, are basically limited to – or worse, content with – reading PowerPoint slides (largely created by someone else) to the students, telling sea/war stories (which some students far prefer to rigorous, guided discussion), and allowing the students to chat with each other in a completely unstructured manner in the name of "adult learning" among "peers."[35] (In fact, some military faculty insist on discussions of "andragogy" – adult learning – rather than the more common term "pedagogy" – youth learning – regarding the PME students. While there are clearly differences, the insistence largely stems from the notion that the students are "peers.") In my supervisory role as department chair, I observed more than a few military faculty in the classroom who regarded asking the seminar what they thought about the topic in hand and then sitting back in a thoughtful pose, occasionally offering a nod or a prod, as "teaching."

Some PME institutions, or departments within institutions, have instituted a practice of hiring military retirees and then requiring them to obtain a doctoral degree. The intended benefits are two-fold: a certain number of faculty holding doctoral degrees are needed for accreditation purposes so it helps check that box. And theoretically, completing a doctoral program requires an individual to conduct rigorous research and synthesize complex arguments, as well as strengthen the person's capacity in their subject matter expertise and hence their ability to teach and be part of the academic profession. The problem is that there is rarely any specification as to what type of doctorate is obtained, or subject matter. Geographical location – the program closest to home so an individual can attend at night – often determines what program is pursued, and often means that the degree obtained has little relationship to what the individual teaches. Further, civilian academia is not above creating or tailoring graduate programs to meet the quick-and-easy needs of the military; creating advanced education programs where overviews are substituted for depth because expediency is key.

Finally, many military faculty attend doctoral programs but see attaining a doctorate as a capstone professional rank, rather than the start of a new career. This is not unreasonable; it is natural to invest more in a first career than a second. But for the academics, this is their first career and their primary identity as professionals, and because of differences in how each culture works, differences arise over how they view education.

There were a number of military retirees on the faculty enrolled in area doctoral programs as a condition of employment when I arrived in Newport as the new department chair in 2002. I soon stopped that requirement. When I recruited a military retiree, it was because they were not only outstanding teachers, but also had a particular area of expertise that could be nurtured without a degree and often had already shown interest in scholarly activity. They had demonstrated potential. Attending a night doctoral program meant that I did not have the individual's full attention for several years (some never finished) and I saw no correlation between second-career academic degrees and whether an individual actually transitioned into becoming a scholar and educator rather than simply continuing their military job in civilian clothes. Regardless of whether they had or obtained higher degree, some retired military faculty developed into valuable faculty members, others did not, just like civilian academic faculty.

At the Air War College there is a similarly growing group of those known as "hybrid" faculty. Dan Hughes explains:

> These have obtained doctoral degrees, at full pay and all expenses, then serve first as colonels and then as civilians upon retirement. A wide variety of graduate schools give them favored treatment so they can complete their degrees in as little as three years. The Army War College leads the way in this program of selective breeding, but the Air University is attempting to catch up in all of

its schools. These ersatz civilians normally are quite deficient in the breadth and depth of their knowledge but lack nothing in self-confidence. They usually acquire none of the ethos of academe. They should not be regarded as civilian professors in the sense that Congress has intended when establishing guidelines for percentages of non-military faculty in the military schools. Management is imperious to the extent to which these colonels undermine the cultural and intellectual diversity of the faculties in these schools, but welcomes them because they are easily controlled and are fully socialized into the military approach to the education and training. For the Air Force, these "colonel-doctors" constitute the ideal "civilian" faculty members. While career officers, they have sufficient "academic stink" to legitimize their civilian faculty status. They are "team players."[36]

To War College administrators, anybody with a doctoral degree is interchangeable with anybody else with a doctoral degree, which is like saying that there is no difference between a naval aviator with 600 traps on an aircraft carrier and someone who just got a pilot's license for a Cessna. For academics, a doctoral degree is akin to being commissioned; the beginning of a career, not an end state. But the more retired military doctoral degrees there are, the more the voices of those arguing for education rather than training can be drowned out.

Civilian academics and practitioners

During a heated meeting at the Naval War College where the faculty rank policy was being discussed, the civilian faculty chairs said we felt such a policy was necessary for getting top recruits. The president asked us to explain. His concern was genuine and appreciated. It is also indicative that most PME administrators have no understanding whatsoever of the academic world, even though they work in, and are leaders of, academic institutions. For some individuals, like this president, that was a concern he sought to rectify. For others, it is not a concern at all.

The issues we raised to the admiral were several, including recruitment timing, advertising, faculty expectations, and risk. I have already outlined faculty expectations in terms of academic freedom, a rank and promotion system, and time to pursue their individual professional careers. The other issues deserve at least brief attention as well.

For example, the standard academic calendar runs from September to June, though some schools start in August and end in May. That means academics sign contracts for those periods. Academic recruitment normally is in the fall, toward contracts being signed January–March for the following academic year. Trying to hire academics "out of cycle" means that a large portion of potential candidates, particularly the best candidates, will be unavailable.

Nevertheless, it was not unusual at the Naval War College that department chairs be told (in February, for example) that they had only a few months to hire multiple new faculty, which immediately meant that hiring would be from a much smaller pool than was desirable. Further, who was viable within that pool was also always a quandary. A brand new twenty-something Ph.D. was sometimes not suitable – or accepted – in a classroom of forty-something military officers. So, we were looking for mature, experienced, successful academics in security studies willing to come to an institution where they will live by ambiguous, tentative rules and not have tenure. That was sometimes a hard sell, and we consequently lost many candidates.[37]

Even advertisements for faculty positions can be deterrents. They are often crafted in ways more suitable to hiring a Pentagon staff position than an educator, using lingo either meaningless or scary to civilian academics. Typically, they include provisions such as:

> This appointment is governed by provisions of 10 USC 7478 as delegated by the Secretary of the Navy, and the regulations of the U.S. Office of Personnel Management which apply to "Excepted" appointments under Schedule A. For the successful candidate, the initial term of appointment is expected to be four years in length with provision for renewal dependent on level of performance.[38]

Though overall the ad content has improved in recent years, as soon as some of the best faculty candidates get to the "three- or four-year contract" portion, they move on.

Further, when academics leave civilian academia to join PME they often do so at their peril, as academia is not always likely to welcome them back if things do not work out. When I left the Florida University system to join the faculty at the Air War College, a colleague stated simply, "So you're going to the dark side." There is an assumption, often (but not always) built on false assumptions, that PME is staffed entirely with right-wing, conservative faculty who are anathema to liberal civilian academics, and that there is no academic freedom or even academic rigor, just the spouting of military jargon.

Publishing a book through Columbia University Press as a PME faculty member, for example, I was told that it would have to go through a more rigorous editorial review because the editorial committee saw that I was from a PME institution. Part of their skepticism about my work and credentials was based on a prejudicial disinclination to work with the military. Part, however, was also legitimately fostered by coming into contact with PME faculty at various places and encountering faculty with full professor titles, yet having little recent or even *any* academic work to their credit. Civilian academics know generally what has been required of a full professor at civilian institutions to achieve full professor status, but the same is not true about PME institutions, which often grant rank based on prior military service or to civilians based on longevity.

While academics in PME who maintain an active professional life may be able to leave in the future, opportunities diminish as they rise in rank and there are fewer and fewer senior civilian positions available. All of this complicates recruiting and retaining academics for PME.

There is, however, a surprising number of top notch civilian academics at the War Colleges. Howard Wiarda specifically cites the individuals he worked with in the mid-1990s, in very complimentary terms:

> Quite a stellar faculty. All Ph.D.s; all with degrees from quite good places. If one considers only the comparative politics, IR [international relations], foreign policy faculties, this was as good a group as almost anywhere in the country.[39]

Ten years ago, the Strategy and Policy Department at the Naval War College was similarly comprised of top scholars like George Baer, Michael Handel, David Kaiser, and Bill Fuller – all since retired or passed away – who built a curriculum that has served as the basis for analogous courses at places like the University of Pennsylvania and Yale. A student writing about his War College experience online went out of his way to praise faculty like Jiri Valenta, Vernon Aspaturian, and

Robert Bathurst.[40] These individuals, however, came to the War College *after* careers in academia, and continued to be active scholars while War College faculty. They were not building their careers subject to a contract system and thus were far more insulated from institutional pressure to cater to the students.

Today, there are many new and long-time civilian academic War College faculty who maintain active lives as scholars, through pockets of internal scholarship and through external organizations such as the Carnegie Council, the Atlantic Council, and the Foreign Policy Institute. From the Naval War College, Derek Reveron is a contributing editor to *New Atlanticist,* and Nick Gvosdev has a weekly column in *World Politics Review*. In the case of the Naval War College, some of this is helped by its fortunate location in New England. My colleague Tom Nichols held a three-year research fellowship at Harvard's Kennedy School, and Tom and I have taught courses for Harvard Extension and Summer School for many years (for which the Harvard Extension School dean thanked the NWC president in a 2009 letter). As just a few other examples of NWC faculty outreach, Mary Raum has spoken at the Harvard Kennedy School; Toshi Yoshihara, Jim Holmes, and Andrew Erickson have given presentations for the Harvard Extension International Relations Club; and James Kraska has spoken to the MIT Security Studies Program. The benefits of these interactions go both ways: NWC faculty provide lectures on specialized topics or participate in workshops, and have the opportunity to network with others in their fields.

At least at the Naval War College, a tipping point of understanding regarding what scholars need to thrive and remain active has been reached. However, many faculty are still unwilling to trust that capricious administrators won't change the standards again, toward measuring the rigor of the curriculum in page counts for student readings, and productivity by how early a professor arrived at his or her office and how late they stay.

Part of that concern stems from an increasing tendency to hire more practitioners – those with long careers in, most-often, government diplomatic or security-related posts – rather than academics, to be blended into the civilian faculty mix. Cynthia Watson states that at National War College:

> While there are a couple of faculty members who are pure academics, the fear has always been that someone without expertise in

government would be at a distinct disadvantage in seminar discussions with NWC students who put such emphasis on practical experience.[41]

Practitioners, however, come with their own set of issues.

Practitioners, many of whom hold doctoral degrees, are increasingly included in PME faculties for the specialization and experience they can bring, and they are especially important in War Colleges because of the increased need to pay attention to interagency issues. Afghanistan has clearly demonstrated that the military will not be operating alone in the future, but must be able to work with other departments. Practitioners come in different varieties: ambassadors and cabinet secretaries have long been coveted by universities as prized assets, because of the breadth of their knowledge and their vast experience. Sometimes, they have worked directly for the President of the United States, coordinating activities in an entire country. They understand and appreciate the value of subject matter experts, having had to work with and sometimes rely on them.

Civilian institutions, however, have made particular accommodations for practitioners to distinguish them from academic faculty. Ambassador R. Nicholas Burns, for example, is a Professor of *Practice* of Diplomacy and International Relations at the Harvard Kennedy School, acknowledging his rank is not academic, but in recognition of his State Department and governmental experience. Former Pakistani Ambassador to the United States, Husain Haqqani, is an associate professor at Boston University. Evan Hillebrand is an associate professor of geoeconomics at the University of Kentucky after serving 30 years in high-level positions with the Central Intelligence Agency. So the most senior academic ranks are not conferred lightly, and designations of "Professor of Practice" are increasingly common to acknowledge that one set of credentials does not equate to another, while respecting both.

But again, military institutions believe that military expertise is interchangeable with any level of other expertise. There is an old joke, for example, told by State Department personnel. An ambassador and a general are talking. The general confidently says, "You know, I think I'd make a good ambassador when I retire." The ambassador replies with equal swagger: "And I think I'd make a good general after I leave the State Department." The flabbergasted general replies, "But years of experience and knowledge are required to qualify for that kind of position and responsibility!" The ambassador replies simply: "Exactly."

Former congressional staff members with experience on Capitol Hill can be valuable catches as faculty, as well as private think-tank specialists and others from the Defense Department and elsewhere who have substantial depth in areas of interest to the War Colleges, and demonstrate their intent to continue substantive pursuits. But PME should be selective. As one of my colleagues has said, you can pull up a minivan to any metro stop within a five-mile radius of the Pentagon or any D.C. government department and fill it with self-described high-level "practitioners" any time or day of the week. This group has spent their careers as bureaucrats, sometimes in narrow fields, sometimes as a jack-of-all-trades, who rarely have had experience making actual policy. While practitioners can bring crucially needed "fresh eyes" to the PME system, being neither academic nor military, their long-term value as faculty members may be undermined by a limited understanding of the academic enterprise of graduate military education. This can lead to problems.

At the National War College, according to both Cynthia Watson and Howard Wiarda, most of the academic faculty are practitioners rather than academics. Wiarda provides his perspective on the employment of that hiring model:

> Most of the Ph.D.s at the War College were not true, university-based academics; rather, they were recruited mainly out of government service ranks (CIA, DOD, State, Congressional staff) and not from academia. That means that, while often quite brilliant, they did not usually have strong research, teaching or publication records. Their degrees, like mine, were mostly from good public state universities, not prestigious Ivy League institutions. And because they came out of careers in government service, they were used to working in large public bureaucracies, taking orders, and subordinating their private interests to the good of the institution.[42]

Especially in Washington, the primary qualifications for a faculty position may be geographic proximity and ability to network with former colleagues.[43] Once hired, while often able to offer valuable substantive expertise in particular substantive areas, practitioners are understandably less able to mentor faculty, more process-oriented and less understanding of faculty governance issues or professional development needs. This difference in background becomes especially important when practitioners become PME administrators.

Department chairs in civilian academia typically take the position of chair because it is their turn and obligation. They do not see it as a hierarchical position of control or "being the boss," but rather something like the managing partner in a law firm; someone who, of necessity, must manage the administrative responsibilities among a group of professionals. Practitioners can have very different views. They can tend toward treating faculty as staff – understandable, as that is who they are used to dealing with – and have little or no experience with academic practices. Consequently, however, they show little understanding of the idea that part of their job is to advocate for the faculty to the higher administration. Further, practitioners, like the military, are hierarchical, and because they therefore want to please their bosses, they are often unwilling to speak truth to power.

Institutional administrators

Administrators have key roles in faculty hiring and consequently in perpetuating the training approach to education at the War Colleges. The War Colleges are all headed by an active-duty general officer, under the title of Commandant or President.[44] Howard Wiarda states that there were two types of commandants at National War College.[c]

> The one type is a general or admiral who is content with his career, ready to retire, and is only looking for a quiet pasture where he can live comfortably, maybe play a little golf or tennis, and go quietly to live on his pension. The other type is feisty, wants to make his mark, and thinks he can remake NWC in his image. The second type is often arrogant, likes to order people around, and seldom has much use for the curriculum or the civilian faculty...[45]

---

c NWC, as used by Wiarda, references the National War College; elsewhere NWC references the Naval War College, with "National" used to designate the National War College.

A variant on these types that I have known is the commandant/ president who sees heading a War College as a stepping-stone to a next "star." (Generals and admirals initially are granted one "star" and, as they get promoted, can be granted up to four.) War College presidents are usually two-star generals or admirals. Those who have been led to expect further promotion usually maintain a low profile and avoid controversy until that third star arrives. Three Naval War College presidents in the past ten years have been awarded a third star; two have gone directly from their Naval War College assignment to being the Navy Inspector General.

George Reed, having served in the military and being an academic, also shares his perspective on what he describes as "an important variable in the quality of professional military education:"

> The services have made both inspired and miserable choices in selecting those who serve as chief executives of their War Colleges. Selection for two stars or more is not sufficient qualification on its own to serve as a college president, even a War College. Neither should it be a consolation prize for those who are not selected for combat command. As a positive and rare exemplar consider Major General Gregg Martin, who served as both a student and faculty member at the Army War College before assuming duties as commandant. I will say the same about lesser administrative roles as well. Successful completion of brigade, ship or squadron command does not inherently qualify a person to be a deputy commandant, chief of staff, provost, dean or department chair. Such key positions require...demonstrated ability in academic settings.[46]

Reed's last point is particularly important and almost always ignored. Over the course of 20 years, I have known only four individuals to hold administrative positions in PME institutions who actually had experience in academia, either as an administrator or as a faculty member who has sat on hiring, tenure, and curriculum committees. Three were at the department level, one was a dean. The dean left his position (and the institution) after a year or so, tired of being continually blocked by the retired military in his efforts to instill academic standards and processes in the institution.

It is important to make a distinction between individuals who have experience in such academic tasks as hiring, tenure, and curriculum development, from those with advanced degrees. Judith Stiehm, for example, describes the composition of the faculty at the National War College, stating that, "The civilian faculty all held Ph.D.s, all had taught at major civilian universities, and all but one had worked in the federal government."[47] That does not, however, necessarily mean that any of those individuals have academic experience relevant for academic administration, as they may well have held adjunct teaching positions while federal employees. They are, accordingly to both Wiarda and Watson, practitioners. Similarly, some military administrators pursue advanced degrees while holding administrative positions at the War Colleges. A National Defense University president pursued and received a doctorate in education, for example, while serving as president. Degrees, however, while potentially important for scholarly growth, do not inherently equate to academic experience.

Personally, I have worked for eight commandants/presidents in three PME institutions (two War Colleges), of all types. One individual went so far as to change all the art work in the building to battle scenes to be more in line with the "warrior" environment he felt appropriate. One tried very hard to make real changes toward an educational model of teaching and merit-based hiring, only to find himself consistently butting heads with the retired military cabal that surrounded him, and who knew they could outlast him – as they did. Many are familiar to faculty only through the stars on their uniform as they pass in the hallway, as the presidents and commandants often become familiar with a small group of individuals and interact mostly with them.

The power of the commandants/presidents can be directly related to how big and entrenched their civilian staff are, and how willing they are to take on the staff if the staff opposes them. In one case at the Naval War College, for example, a meeting was held where the topic pitted the academic department chairs against the retired-military administrators. The president sided with the department chairs but, understanding the power of the retired military that would clearly outlast him, openly turned to the provost and asked, "Should I bother making this decision or are you just going to ignore it and overturn it the day I leave?"

Sadly, burgeoning administrative staff positions – the fleet of deans, assistant deans, associate deans, associate provosts, program directors, special advisors, and "professors" with various titles, whose duties are unclear and who hold senior titles (not to mention six-figure salaries) and influence institutional policy – are not unique to PME. Carl Elliot's *Wall Street Journal* review of Benjamin Ginsberg's 2011 book *The Fall of the Faculty* succinctly describes the problem:

> Mr. Ginsberg argues that universities have degenerated into poorly managed pseudo-corporations controlled by bureaucrats so far removed from research and teaching that they have barely any idea what these activities involve. He attacks everyone – from overpaid presidents and provosts down through development officers, communications specialist and human-resource staffers – but he reserves his most bitter scorn for the midlevel "associate deans" and "assistant deans" who often have the most direct control over the faculty. Mr. Ginsberg refers to them as 'deanlets,' but at my institution they are often called 'ass.deans.'[48]

Presidential candidate Newt Gingrich even commented on the trend in November 2011, in response to a question about federal student aid, stating that "by 2014 there will be one administrator for every teacher on college campuses in the United States."[49]

Problems with an expanding administration in academia are exacerbated in PME. The resultant "bewildering" menu of programs and courses, and general chaos, that Ginsberg says are created by these middle managers in civilian academia bears a striking resemblance to a proliferation of missions at the War Colleges, all draining funds from core departments, and all requiring more and more retired military to run them, but with one key difference. The "deanlets" at the War Colleges are not "removed" from their original responsibilities in teaching and research; with few exceptions they have little or no background in education or academia in the first place.

Often PME administrative jobs are filled in questionable ways. Some are created – a sudden need identified – just as loyal individuals retire; others are filled without fully advertising the positions, or as the result of "worldwide" searches that produce a particular officer – close to retirement and who happens to be sitting down the hall – as the only viable candidate.

At the Naval War College, according to the Faculty Handbook, "Department Chairs and other key administrative personnel are selected by the Provost. Appointments to these positions are normally for a four-year term and may be renewed no more than once."[50] While the letter of that policy is largely adhered to, the spirit is not. Rarely do administrators return to positions in the faculty after their tenure as administrators, as is often the norm in academia. Rather, the title of their position is simply changed (an associate dean becomes an associate provost, but does the same job) or they are moved to a different – sometimes newly created – administrative position through a non-competitive process. Hiring rigor is possible, though, and in some cases a competitive process is used.

Faculty hired for my department (only the provost has hiring authority, so I would make recommendations to the provost) at the Naval War College while I was chair, for example, went through a rigorous, inclusive process. Files were first screened by a faculty committee with recommendations sent to me (and I also reviewed all files separately), and an evaluation of how each candidate met the stated criteria was discussed by the committee. Candidates brought in for interviews over a day-and-a-half period had at least one informal meal with the faculty, possibly two, two meetings with me, and meetings with all interested faculty members. The candidate then gave a presentation to the faculty and addressed questions, much as they would have to do teaching a seminar. Everyone had input.

I have found processes for hiring War College administrators, however, sometimes wildly varying from practices that are the norm in civilian academic institutions. In academia, the norm is to have a clear job description, with qualifications stated in the advertisement, and then a discussion within the recruitment committee on the strengths and weaknesses of each candidate in meeting the qualifications. Votes would be taken in small groups (as in a dean or provost search), and never would seniors and subordinates both be included on those committees, to avoid having the subordinate having to vote in potential opposition to their own boss. Nor would a faculty member vote on someone who was previously their supervisor, to potentially make a subordinate their boss, or vote on a higher rank than one for which they would qualify. Faculty involvement in selecting individuals who will govern the institution is considered valuable. While things can certainly go haywire in this process as well, the idea is that faculty are professional peers, and having everyone feel they have had input into the selection of their leadership builds a cooperative spirit.

By contrast, I was on the committee for selecting both a provost and academic dean at the Naval War College. While the process for selecting the provost was extremely abbreviated – finalist interviews consisted of a single one-hour meeting with the recruitment committee only – it was a merit-based selection process. The process used for selecting the dean of academics, however, after two prior failed searches (I was a candidate in the second) involved what I considered such irregularities in process and committee composition that I resigned from the recruitment committee.

There was no clear job description, especially important since the provost is the dean of the faculty (not the norm in academia, but it does happen), so job responsibilities for the dean of academics were unclear, which made evaluating qualifications impossible. "Being a team player" was the guidance for candidate selection given to the committee. My request that candidates speak to the faculty and/or meet with the faculty as part of the process was turned down; only a faculty committee selected by the provost would be involved, and they met with each candidate for an hour, compared with junior faculty who are interviewed for a day or more. Even in the selection of my replacement as department chair, only one member of the departmental faculty (of almost 50) was included on the hiring committee selected by the provost.

Dan Hughes provides an interesting hiring vignette for an Air War College department chair illustrating how little merit and qualifications can come into play:

> This person, retiring from a similar position at one of the other War Colleges, applied for a job as a department chair at the Air War College. During the public portion of the interview, he reached into his briefcase with great flourish and triumphantly pulled out three books that he announced would be the core of what he would use to teach strategy. When asked to compare the books' views on a particular subject, he had to admit that he had not actually read any of them. This same person offered the opinion that a professor's fund of knowledge peaks upon finishing graduate school and declines thereafter. As ridiculous as this episode was, the dean, also a retired colonel-doctor, nevertheless wanted to hire this person as a department chair.[51]

The educational goals of the institutions are undermined by this exclusion of the faculty from governance decisions. It is not at all unusual for a kind of unholy alliance to be formed between the retired military and the civilian academic faculty who are not professionally active. Both are supportive of the status quo, training-style approach to education.

As War College administrations grow larger, they increasingly become preoccupied with the inherent bureaucratic goal of self-perpetuation of their jobs. This was empirically demonstrated in 2004 when the Naval War College hired a well-known consulting firm (at a very high price) to consider institutional efficiency and return on investment at Newport. The consultants immediately noted the remarkable and sudden high growth of administrative positions, though the briefers (who are always looking to please the customer and so be awarded a follow-on contract) were later persuaded to omit that finding from the final report. The study was relegated to a drawer and never seen again.

The result of administrators imposing often arbitrary personnel and professional policies on what is intended as a collegial body is that, from whatever background, faculty on the contract treadmill end up trying to game the system. They will hypocritically pick and choose when they want to be considered as federal employees and when they want to be respected as academics. When told that they should match the productivity of their peers at other institutions, they claim such demands are impossible for a mere federal worker. But when they want to take time off, seek funds for academic travel, or devote time to their own pursuits, they stand on their educational credentials. If faculty want to reap the benefits of the kind of treatment they feel is due to them as scholars, then they must be held to the same scholarly standards found at similar educational institutions. Where their ability and willingness to stay actively engaged in their profession beyond the parameters of PME becomes evident is in curriculum development, which is the subject of the next chapter.

5 The curriculum

Moving toward intellectual agility

> Sir, that was the best lecture I've ever heard anywhere on any subject. But unfortunately, it didn't teach me jack-squat about how to take that hill.
>
> A Naval War College student to a faculty member

A strong faculty can execute almost any curriculum, but even the best teachers cannot overcome poor materials and turn mediocrity into excellence. Although organized differently and called by various departmental names, all War Colleges teach the same categories of material, because they are dictated by the JPME guidelines. In general, these categories include critical thinking, military history, leadership, national security affairs, and joint military operations. They are all supposed to be taught with a strategic focus and at a level where students are required to "apply, analyze, evaluate, and synthesize" knowledge and concepts. Teaching at the strategic level means focussing students away from the tactical and operational levels of military operations with which they are comfortable, and into areas with which they are largely inexperienced and have little or no prior foundational knowledge.

Consequently, teaching economic, historical, political, and geopolitical concepts at the "apply, analyze, evaluate and synthesize" level to individuals largely from technical and engineering backgrounds can sometimes be akin to teaching engineering to an Early English literature major. Trying to have a seminar-style discussion about the future of NATO with individuals who have no idea when or why NATO was created is a challenge.

Curriculum development

David Maxwell, from the Foreign Service School at Georgetown and a retired Army Special Forces officer, extoled on the value of a common, or core, curriculum in January 2012 article in *Small Wars Journal.*[1] In fact, the "common curriculum" already taught among the PME schools and within each PME department is a major difference between PME education and graduate education at civilian institutions, with decidedly mixed results. In civilian academic institutions, individual faculty develop and execute their courses in their entirety. PME subject matter is based on the Officer Professional Military Education Policy (OPMEP)[2] from the office of the Chairman of the Joint Chiefs of Staff.

OPMEP "learning area" requirements[3] provide the basic guidance for what is to be included in the curriculum. Specifically, these include: (1) National Security Strategy; (2) National Military Strategy and Organization; (3) Joint Warfare, Theater Strategy and Campaigning; (4) National and Joint Planning Systems and Processes; (5) Integration of Joint, Interagency and Multinational Campaigns; (6) Information Operations, C2 and Battlespace Awareness; and (7) Joint Strategic Leadership Development. Each of these areas then has multiple subsections. Learning areas 1, 2 and 7 most obviously allow for broadening educational goals beyond operations, though there are opportunities elsewhere as well. For example, Learning Area 3e reads: "Apply an analytic framework that incorporates the role that factors such as geopolitics, geostrategy, society, culture, and religion play in shaping the desired outcomes of policies, strategies and campaigns in the joint, interagency, and multinational arena."[4] The breadth of that learning area is especially significant.

Having a common, core curriculum is a good news/bad news story. It is good news in that without the requirement to do so, it is questionable whether or not anything beyond military operations would be taught at War Colleges, so the OPMEP serves to broaden War College curricula. But whether those responsible for OPMEP content have an appropriate background for that task is also questionable. A Naval War College administrator, for example, suggested that the OPMEP was written by O-4s and O-5s[a] at the Pentagon who know nothing about

---

a Majors and Lieutenant Colonels in the Army, Air Force and Marines, and Lieutenant Commanders and Commanders in the Navy.

education. They were assigned to a job and carried it out, but with little or no substantive expertise behind their efforts. Their successors continue to update the OPMEP under the same parameters. It seems a fair assumption that Navy medical standards are set by medical professionals; Navy nuclear engineering standards by people with nuclear engineering backgrounds; and Navy flight manuals written by people who have actually flown a plane. Are education standards similarly set by educators, or by random officers and individuals, and similarly executed by such?[b]

When individuals who know little about a subject are assigned responsibility for that subject, they often will default to generalized models. In the case of education that model is Bloom's taxonomy[5] for increasingly cognitive levels of learning, or how people progress from an ability to perform simple tasks to complex ones. Simply stated, the taxonomy states that individuals' abilities progress through six levels of complexity as they learn: knowledge, comprehension, application, analysis, synthesis, and evaluation. You must, for example, *know* information about a subject before you can *analyze* a subject. So to begin, according to the OPMEP the JPME 1 intermediate course is to be taught at the "know and comprehend" levels and the JPME 2 senior course at the "apply, analyze, evaluate and synthesize" levels. But, again, as pointed out by the NWC administrator, how one could be expected to teach a graduate-level course at the "know and comprehend" level (at the intermediate command and staff colleges, not the War Colleges) is baffling to anyone with any experience in education. How students with little or no prior substantive background in the subject material can be expected to jump right to application and analysis – and all succeed in ten months to get a Master's degree – is similarly baffling. Nevertheless, that is the instruction, and the result.

The degree to which individualization in the classroom is allowed or encouraged varies. Sometimes, a set of ready-made PowerPoint slides is provided to the instructor, and little deviation from those slides is expected or encouraged.

---

b   An individual who called me in 2011 about educational policy being considered by the Navy staff said that he was a retired intelligence officer with no background in education. In a follow-up call he stated that six Executive Advisory Boards (EAB) had been set up to further consider Navy educational policies. When I asked if any career academics were includes on any of those EABs the answer was: "There are no educators on the boards."

At the Air War College, for example, I was initially hired to teach a hybrid course of political science and defense economics. Soon thereafter my boss, an Air Force colonel, visited my office to ask why I had missed several preparatory workshops for teaching Total Quality Management (TQM), a fad management-efficiency approach based on making cars then popular in DOD. Surprised, I replied that I was a political scientist who knew nothing about TQM, and therefore I hadn't expected that I would be asked to teach it. Not to worry, he explained, none of the faculty knew anything about TQM, but the Air Staff wanted it taught, so we would all be provided with PowerPoint slides to walk through with the students. I would pretend to teach, the students would pretend to learn.

In areas of OPMEP-dictated core curriculum, having a set of ready-made slides provided to instructors often sits well with military faculty unsure of the subject matter and for civilians who do not wish to expand beyond their time-tested teaching notes. Also, pre-packaged notes are the only way to get faculty up to speed on the flavor-of-the-month fads.

One theoretical benefit of a collectively developed curriculum is that sessions are supposed to be developed by experts on the subject, while giving the entire faculty a sense of "buy-in" and engagement. But in practice, expertise is often a secondary consideration, as workload must be fairly distributed (one or two individuals can't do it all) and a large breadth of subjects covered. Each individual faculty member may be responsible for the creation of two or three sessions of a 25-session course. Thus, instant experts must be found. And once a curriculum is developed, the temptation grows to resist further change, because it is easier to teach a roster of agreed-upon issues than to engage in continual and intellectually taxing change. But whereas some departmental curricula can become moribund due to ease and likability, others suffer from exactly the opposite problem, constant churn.

A War College curriculum ought to strive for relevance, but this should not mean constant curriculum churn for non-substantive reasons. Too often, however, the common curriculum becomes subject to internal institutional politics. Faculty and administrators pay careful attention to which courses have the most time allotted to them during the academic year – as an indicator of importance – and of course, to the most important institutional metric of success: whether the students "like" courses.[c] Turf battles between departments and institutional demands for student satisfaction can result in a constant demand for change, some major, but more often minor. Hours can be spent word-smithing the title of a 90-minute seminar session, considering and reconsidering the order and font of PowerPoint slides, and making the case to administrators that all course material is immediately relevant to the entire student body – or at least more so than what is being taught in other departments. Buzzwords like "synergy" become guidance for curriculum development, often insisted upon by administrators with little or no experience in curriculum development. Often, as well, War College administrators try to anticipate the interests of the next president or commandant, directing faculty to emphasize areas (often already covered) like net-centric warfare, China, or economics. Since curriculum space is zero-sum, though, putting something in, means taking something else out.

Additionally, primacy given to "teamwork" at the War Colleges is taken to counterproductive lengths. One well-meaning Naval War College president wanted to hold a meeting on developing a new inter-mediate course and to invite much of the building administrative staff. He felt that everyone should have the opportunity to provide input. The academic department chairs adamantly and collectively objected, noting that the officer in charge of building maintenance or the comp-troller should have no role in curriculum development. This had never occurred to the president. Fortunately, however, when presented with the rationale for having the curriculum developed *only* by those with subject matter expertise and who would be executing the curriculum, the president changed his position on the need for building-wide buy-in and a show of all-hands teamwork. He left it to the faculty. The larger irony, however, is that while academic faculty are deliberately kept out of academic administration decisions, as with the writing of the OPMEP, non-experts are commonly considered qualified to partic-ipate in academic and curricular decisions.

How much "help" a War College gets from service leadership is also sometimes a problem. At the Air War College, beyond trendy initiatives like TQM, too often there were flavor-of-the-month directives sent from the Air Staff regarding what specific sessions should be included

---

c As with any survey, asking the right question is key. Great care is often taken to phrase student evaluation questions with enough ambiguity to guarantee a favorable outcome.

in the curriculum. (I recall, for example, a mandate for including a class session on the environment and the commander – basically, cleaning up environmental waste when a base was closing.) The result was a curriculum sometimes so disjointed that faculty attempting to coherently execute it were described by a visiting professor, well known in the security studies field, from the University of Alabama, as "dead men walking."

Former Marine Corps Command and Staff College faculty member Mark Moyer wrote about the difficulties creating a new curriculum in 2009. "These schools are constantly receiving bright ideas from outsiders about what they should teach, and they usually believe those outsiders aren't qualified to make impositions on their curriculum."[6] Moyer is correct that faculty do resist externally imposed changes to the curriculum. That can be good when changes would result in a curriculum made disjointed by fads, but bad when important new topics should displace entrenched ideas in the curriculum that are not as relevant but with which the students and the faculty are comfortable. Ideally, a balance should be struck between an enduring curriculum, on one hand, and relevance and timeliness where appropriate.

The PME system, perhaps more frequently than at civilian institutions, is able to insert material into the curriculum very quickly. When President Barack Obama issued his Strategic Defense Guidance in January 2012, for example, it was being read and discussed in seminars by students at the Naval War College within a week of issue – as it should have been. But care also needs to be taken that courses don't evolve into current events seminars.

To its benefit, the Naval War College curriculum has been fortunate in not being tossed and turned by such specific directives. Newport, however, also has been careful to keep an appropriate "pulse" on Navy and national needs. For example, by 2004 it was clear that any real victory in Iraq was going to require more than bullets and tanks. Consequently, DOD mandated that PME include consideration of social science subjects beyond what had been the norm. The mandate was part of a DOD-wide effort called Countering Ideological Support for Terrorism (CIST). In Newport, regional studies, including religion and culture, history, economics, and globalization were recognized as areas about which officers had to be more knowledgeable to be successful in their new, increasingly complex environment. We also added a case on nuclear strategy, correctly anticipating that the Defense Department would increasingly want to see this subject reflected in the curriculum of the War Colleges. More civilian academic experts in expanded fields were required, and hired, to address these topics.

Additionally, the Chief of Naval Operations wanted more emphasis on "leadership" in the curriculum some years back. So in 2004, when the Naval War College was engaged in a two-year effort to develop a new, distinctly different ILC from the SLC (previously, both courses had been targeted at the senior level, as naval officers rarely had the opportunity for both) particular focus was put on the subject of leadership. Faculty members took the opportunity to meet with numerous admirals and generals in Newport and Washington, toward getting an idea of what kind of leadership studies they felt would be useful. Their consistent advice was to make students understand that leadership at strategic levels involves more than being adept in one narrow operational field and instead, being able to deal with a multitude of issues largely out of their control.

Faculty, including experts with extensive expertise in areas including organizational management and civil–military relations, then developed a leadership seminar. The students read a breadth of case studies, including perennial favorites such as Ulysses S. Grant and Robert E. Lee, Dwight Eisenhower, and Hyman Rickover, but also including individuals such as Nelson Mandela and F. W. DeKlerk, Indira Ghandi, and former IBM chief Louis Gerstner.

These are the kinds of courses military officers are unlikely to get at a civilian school. Not surprisingly, the students are still sometimes uncomfortable with both the material and the "figure it out yourself" seminar approach used in this course. Most prefer – at least initially – what a colleague who had taught at the Army War College described as the three-step Army approach to teaching: tell the students what you're going to tell them, tell them, tell them what you told them. Some, however, see it for the unique opportunity it provides.

Part of the difficulty with PME curriculum development, and execution, is the inverse of what usually happens in academia, where everyone is a specialist, and often in very narrow fields. In PME, not all faculty (and even fewer administrators) are classically trained in disciplines that require broad, analytical thinking. So when they become responsible for developing a graduate level multidisciplinary curriculum, it is not surprising that many revert to a process-focussed orientation, at a very basic level. Consequently, some faculty, quite understandably, doubt the veracity of calling the result a graduate program.

Both Howard Wiarda and Dan Hughes are skeptical about the level of the core curriculum at the National War College and the Air War College, respectively. Wiarda says:

> NWC directors consistently argue, for prestige purposes, that their program is at a master's degree level and they have both sought and achieved accreditation at that level and, from time to time, offered a master's degree in international security policy. However, my experience at the War College is that the courses, readings, requirements, grading, etc. are really at the level of a junior-senior undergraduate course in international relations.[7]

Similarly, Dan Hughes describes the curriculum at the Air War College as, "...courses that are assemblages of basic approaches based on undergraduate-level readings."[8]

Even graduate level material was not, in some cases, taught at a graduate level. For years at the Naval War College, the faculty would read seminal security studies articles by Samuel Huntington, Graham Allison, and others, and then provide three- or four-page *summaries* to the students in lieu of having them read the full articles themselves. When neither the faculty nor the students have much background in security studies, the propensity to take a short-cut approach to education is understandable. But analysis requires that the students do their own reading, and figure things out for themselves.

Appropriately, War Colleges focus less on theory than do counterpart civilian institutions. In PME, every attempt is made to maximize student learning experiences through case studies, seminar discussions, and other methods known from civilian professional schools (rather than purely academic programs) to tap into adult student strengths whenever possible. Nevertheless, some individuals do not see these efforts as sufficient.

James Schneider, a former faculty member at the Army's School for Advanced Military Studies, professed in Tom Ricks' blog in 2011 that the teaching of strategy in the military is even worse than the already-skeptical Ricks believed. He specifically targets teaching methods promoted by civilian academics as problematic. He says:

[T]he teaching of strategy is taught primarily by civilian academics using essentially the same eighteenth century methods of instruction designed for clerics. The university system, especially as it relates to the humanities, has totally overlooked the *clinical method of instruction* that revolutionized medicine in the nineteenth century with the invention of the teaching hospital.[9] [author's emphasis]

Schneider is not alone in his views. Naval War College professor Tom Hone argued similarly for more of a professional school approach to PME in a widely circulated email later published on the USNI blog. He compares the needs and approaches of PME to medical and law schools, saying:

But there is often a great difference between an educational institution such as a well known liberal arts college and a professional school. Indeed, one of the criticisms often leveled against professional schools of law and medicine is that their programs are too narrow, or too technical, and that therefore they really don't prepare tomorrow's doctors and lawyers to learn as they progress through their careers.[10]

But what could Schneider and Hone mean? First, what are the "often-leveled" criticisms Professor Hone mentions of law and medical schools as being too "technical"? The tax code and neurosurgery are inherently technical, but even tax lawyers and neurosurgeons grapple with the larger issues of their profession, including ethics, during their years of schooling. Neurosurgeons are educated regarding the body's "systems," not just trained in their specialty. Who would want to be operated on by a brain surgeon who has no understanding of the circulatory system? Tax lawyers must be educated on general areas of law such as jurisdiction, or their specialized knowledge of the tax code can be worthless. The whole enterprise of education is *how* to think – and be able to analyze complex issues – rather than *what* to think, especially when lives are at stake.

PME academic leaders are too often told that military education is "different" and has a kind of "otherness" that academics need to accept and appreciate, or they should leave the PME world. "Love it or leave it," however, is not a solution. Striving for excellence is the better option.

Curriculum execution

Methods of curricular execution, i.e. what teaching methods are used, vary significantly across PME institutions. Three instructions in the required "teacher training," at the Air War College, for example, explained everything I needed to know about its pedagogy. First, never use red ink when grading student papers: direct criticism of military professionals would be insulting. Second, never cold-call a student: not knowing the answer would be demeaning. Third, faculty were classroom "moderators," not teachers. The classroom was for sharing student views, so faculty should speak minimally. This last instruction often resulted in 90-minute sessions where students mostly reinforced each other's views and exchanged dead-wrong information, but this was equated to "education." Though never encouraged to publish at the AWC, I was encouraged to play golf in the Wednesday afternoon student faculty team-building tournaments.

Some schools and departments use a single teacher in the seminar room for each course; others use team instruction where the course teaching load is shared, while others use team instruction with a military moderator and a civilian academic in the same seminar for each session. At the Air War College there was a single faculty member in each seminar, but also a military "seminar director" who, depending on their personality, would either act as a kind of homeroom teacher for students to bring their issues to, or sit in on classes as a faculty watchdog, interrupting, and at times even contradicting, faculty at will.

In some instances a civilian academic is paired with a military officer to provide (in theory) differing perspectives on the subject matter being presented. But does it work? Sometimes. But at other times it appears doubtful. A military faculty member (with several years' teaching experience at a service academy as well) in one department wrote an evaluation (called an After Action Report, or AAR) upon completing a course in another department that used military-civilian teaching teams. He stated:

> From my experience...the military professor is more like a college T.A. (teaching assistant) than an equal member of the teaching team. Our seminar discussions were almost entirely led by the civilian professor, and there seemed to be no added benefit to having an additional professor in the classroom.

Similarly, a student at the Naval War College commented on the same team teaching approach in a December 2011 blog post. He says it results in "a mishmash of officers who are hopelessly outclassed academically by their civilian peers and in some cases are ignored in the classroom by those same peers."[11] Nevertheless, some departments are wedded to this approach. Why?

There are many advantages to team teaching. Team teaching is sometimes supported to share the workload so that the military faculty has less material to master. Additionally, some departments have higher student contact hours than others due to OPMEP requirements, and so the team approach can be useful to avoid faculty burn-out. For Newport faculty who teach both the ILC and the SLC, burn-out can be a serious issue. On a pragmatic level, regarding the all-important student evaluations, evaluating a "team" rather than individuals, and regularly switching the team members, makes it impossible to identify weak teachers, *thereby protecting jobs*. Protecting weak faculty is not a motivation for team teaching that is theoretically possible – it is an approach that has been employed in fact.

The balance between large lectures and seminar discussions also varies, as does the student reading load. Reading assignments range from about 80 pages per night, to other cases where there are a dozen or more readings per session, sometimes in excess of 300 pages per session. Cynthia Watson states that NDU students average 500 pages weekly,[12] and Bradford Lee says NWC students in the Strategy & Policy Department read about 600 pages weekly.[13] Students should have a vigorous reading load. However, for many years in my department at the NWC, we kept data from student evaluations that consistently said the students will read about 80 pages per night. After that, they stop, and many will admit to not completing these large assignments. The faculty AAR succinctly summarized the fiction versus reality of heavy reading loads: "Nearly every student I talked to found a method to read only what they believed was necessary. For our seminar, it was what our teaching team told us to 'focus' on for the week." Perhaps more damning, some faculty members of departments with heavy reading loads privately admit they don't do all the reading either.

The reason for these heavy loads varies. They are often assigned by individuals with particular interests in the (often historical) subject matter, and so feel that every nuance must be explored. Others, perhaps with less depth in the session they are responsible for, are unsure what is relevant so assign quantity to make up for quality. And the safe approach is to assign whatever readings the students have "liked' in the past, and simply add on recent material, as a way of demonstrating "currency." Cumulatively, the readings just increase.

Some institutions and departments use large lectures and readings as the basis for seminar discussions, others rely primarily on readings. There are good reasons for both approaches. When lectures are given to the entire student body by resident professors or invited speakers, they are followed by seminar discussions based on the lecture and the assigned readings. Many resident lecturers are top-notch. Whether the students actually notice, however, is another matter. One term at the Naval War College, many students evaluated a particular lecture as "outstanding", which was interesting since it was canceled due to inclement weather. Lecturing to military officers is a special challenge, as students will be evaluating and "rating" the lecturer, again pertinent in faculty contract renewal. While true at other colleges as well, the basis for the military evaluations can be difficult to anticipate.

A few Air War College students complained bitterly, for example, that I ought not be allowed to lecture after I said on the stage that one of the reasons President Richard Nixon approved the building of the Space Shuttle was for electoral support from aerospace workers in states like Florida and California. They thought it was unpatriotic. Another faculty member was berated for saying that the United States had lost the war in Vietnam.

Wayne Silkett, a former military faculty member and Soviet Foreign Area Officer at the Army War College, conveys a similar situation when he cast doubt on the idea that Americans single-handedly won WWII:

> [A] colleague asked me to give a quick overview of World War II on the Eastern Front. I did so only to have a student storm out to turn me in to the commandant because I had pointed out that the real killing, dying, and destruction in WWII had been on the Eastern Front, which obviously upset his view that it could not be so. Though General Robert Scales was commandant at the time and confirmed that what I had said was true...the student never apologized.[14]

While the students are not hesitant to assail resident faculty speakers whose views do not match their own, external speakers sometimes fare no better, and for good reason.

Invited flag officers and external government practitioners are provided with a topic to speak on, and some give speeches that are useful and even inspiring. Others disregard the request for a subject focus in favor of whatever happens to be on their mind, or a canned speech handed to them on the way to their car or the plane. Some speakers basically invite themselves and administrators feel compelled to oblige to provide them with an audience; this can be a particular problem in the Washington area. Some are, as Judith Stiehm calls them, "scholarly friends" of administrators.[15] The risk of bringing in someone from outside who may or may not speak on the subject requested must be weighed against the value of having "practitioners" supplement the academic curriculum with real-life examples.

When lectures are not used, seminar discussion is theoretically based on the readings. That is the nature of a seminar. But if there is a speaker to rely on as a basis for seminar discussion, student commitment to reading can suffer.

Whether or not students then choose to participate in seminar discussions, and on the subject matter, is another matter. Some departments grade participation, which can lead to participation being forced and mechanical; others do not, which means there is no penalty for never saying a word. There is no totally right answer. Civilian academic institutions face the same dilemma in seminars: drawing out silent students and managing students who simply like to talk, often not enhancing learning. The reality is that a certain amount of in-seminar lecturing is often needed to provide discussion context, because often students, PME or otherwise, do not have a strong background in the subject matter being presented for discussion.

What happens when the seminar door is closed is then the real issue. A former Naval War College faculty member who returned to civilian academia explains the PME seminar situation well:

> Being an effective teacher in PME requires different skills than at a civilian institution; the common syllabi and seminar style of classes where lecturing is discouraged make it possible for anyone to teach PME courses. I don't think that there would be a correlation between the quality of scholars at PME institutions and the

quality of education until the class structure is not simplified to the point that anyone could come in and teach with little or no training or preparation. I was never a fan of the let-them-learn-from-each-other school of thought. After a semester or two of struggling to get productive conversations going by asking questions like "so...what do you folks think of the defense budget process?" I started talking more and more. Teaching, I called it.

"Teaching," however, is not always institutionally encouraged, because not everyone is qualified to do that. In fact, faculty are often referred to as "moderators" rather than "teachers" so as not to offend the student "peers."

Another faculty member, still in residence, suggests a different aspect of the reluctance of some faculty and the institution at large to real "teaching:" senior guys don't want to "spoil the image" for "innocent officers" as to how things get done. A former senior civilian Navy official, for example, stood on stage in Newport and told the student body: "Washington is completely political, *except for the Pentagon.* There are no politics there." [emphasis added] While many of the faculty (and students) initially assumed he was joking, his continued insistence of the purity of "you guys in the audience" made it clear he was not. There seems to be a real tension between "teaching the system" but then worrying about undermining officers' faith in American democracy, though what bad things they worry would happen if the officers were allowed – even encouraged – to peek behind the curtain isn't clear. Thus, teaching "process," is much easier, safer, and able to be accomplished with a prepared set of PowerPoint slides.

Beyond the core curriculum, War College students are also required to take a certain number of electives courses. The rigor of these courses has improved over the years when *Managing Your Money for Dummies* was a required text in a very popular course on financial planning for retirement. Sometimes, too, rather than allowing students to select what areas of study they wish to pursue as an elective, they are placed in a course (which the students refer to as "selectives") determined to be a service "need." Needless to say the students in those courses are often not happy, and that can be reflected in their course evaluations.

The most popular courses are often those where the academic faculty lecture on their niche area and the students listen passively.

These electives are opportunities for faculty not otherwise profession-ally active to develop one set of PowerPoint slides, often on historical subjects not subject to much change, and use them repeatedly, often very well. Another approach is for a faculty member to act as a "host" to a bevy of guest speakers on a particular topic. And for specialized courses, particularly in regional studies, it is not uncommon to bring in academic faculty from area civilian institutions to teach electives.

Students generally like electives, though rigor between them can vary significantly. A sure way to get a class canceled is to require a long paper or more work from the students. The students write a paper of usually eight to ten pages on the topic as part of the course requirement, grades are issued (sometimes pass/fail/high pass) and the box is checked.

Virtually anyone willing to cobble together a syllabus is considered qualified to teach whatever subject they choose, with administrative oversight minimal, and by administrators with often questionable qual-ifications themselves. On one hand, substantively qualified faculty should not be told what to teach by often less-qualified administrators. But when faculty qualifications are weak or dubious, the potential for content issues increases.[16] The Joint Forces Staff College in Norfolk, VA, under the auspices of the National Defense University, found that out after a student objected to material being taught in an elective on "Perspectives on Islam and Islamic Radicalism," taught by a military faculty member, Army Lt. Col. Matthew Dooley, and course materials were posted online by *Wired*.[17] Dooley, a 1994 West Point graduate and Bronze Star winner, was teaching "that America's enemy is Islam in general, not just terrorists, and suggesting that the country might ulti-mately have to obliterate the Islamic holy cities of Mecca and Medina without regard to civilian deaths."[18] The course was subsequently suspended, with Army Chief of Staff General Martin Dempsey saying that it was "totally objectionable" and "against our values."[19]

Finally, no discussion of War College curricula would be complete without mention of the role of sports.

First, PME is perhaps the only graduate program in the United States to include an obligatory sports program, and the level of importance placed on sports at some PME institutions can, at times, surpass the importance placed on academics. In particular, some PME comman-dants place a very high priority on doing well at an annual inter-War College tournament hosted by the Army War College, named after

All-American athlete and gold medal Olympian Jim Thorpe. This multi-day event, held each spring, includes competition in events ranging from track and field to golf and bowling. Forty-something graduate students are expected to train and compete as though they were still 20-something undergraduates in a competition that begins with an opening ceremony enthusiastically described on the Army War College website:

> The colorful ceremony kicks off the sports competition among the students of the nation's War Colleges – Army, Air, National and Industrial College of the Armed Forces. Following the parade of athletes will be the Old Guard's Caisson with its seven Percheron horses, the U.S. Military Academy mules, will be the invocation, singing of the National Anthem a cappella, U.S. Air Force fly over (two F16's), the Presidential Gun Battery will provide honors and open the games, and finally the lighting of the official "Olympic" style torch.[20]

One Air War College student returned and described the competitive events as being dominated by the pervasive smell of Ben-Gay. The Naval War College heretically stopped attending a few years ago after the then-president decided the time and cost involved – and a clear lack of student enthusiasm – were too high to justify participation. An internal "President's Cup" sports competition in Newport fills the sports gap instead, at a much more reasonable level of intensity.

At other schools, however, the importance placed on winning is high. Dan Hughes suggests that Air War College zeal for the Jim Thorpe competition involves not just bragging rights, but can be a way for the commandant to show his disdain for academics:

> The faculties provide coaches, making these schools among the very few graduate schools (if there are any others) whose faculties service in this capacity. The competition, which serves no readily apparent useful purpose for future senior officers, closes the school for three days... Usually about 100 AWC students attend. This is, of course, a questionable use of government funds, but the amount is not terribly large, since the students rides busses for the long trip to Carlisle (15 hours or so). For this chapter's topic, however, the real issue is what goes on for the 150 students or so who remain at Maxwell. The Air War College punishes these students for not

participating in the games. For years the faculty used the term "punish" as a bit of humor, but in 2009 officials at the War College used this term to explain the program to students. The punishment consists of additional courses, called "enrichment electives," which are mandatory for the students. Professors volunteer or are dragooned into teaching courses that lack sufficient value to be taught in the regular elective program but which suffice to avoid giving days off to those students who do not wish to pretend to be athletes or cheerleaders. Designing pseudo-academic courses to punish students for not participating in sports competitions is probably unique in the annals of American graduate education and is a clear statement of what really counts at the Air War College.[21]

While the financial cost of the trip might be low, the opportunity costs spent on weekly athletic practices and the event itself, rather than academic studies, is high.

All graduate programs have intramural programs and encourage *mens sana in sano corpore* (a sound mind in a healthy body). But no one would expect that a Georgetown or Johns Hopkins Master's student should train vigorously for weeks and miss a week of class to compete against Tufts or Yale in touch football. It is simply unprofessional that people in their forties, being paid to study and complete coursework, are expected to do this.

In sum, learning does take place in PME, in different forms and at different levels, but less often than it ought to through challenging students and pushing them out of their comfort zones. Ironically, many War College students have children in college and would be appalled to think that the schools they are paying often very high tuition costs to were developing and executing curriculum with thoughts of student happiness as their primary focus.

So where are the PME "parents?"

Oversight and accreditation

Two bodies, one military and one civilian, are responsible for oversight and accreditation of the War College academic programs. On the military side, there is the Process for Accreditation of Joint Military Education (PAJE). On the civilian side there is a regional accreditation body; for example the New England Association of Schools and

Colleges (NEASC) for the Naval War College, and the Middle States Association of Schools and Colleges for the Army War College. As part of the PAJE process, the DOD internally examines the colleges every six years to "certify" that they are meeting the obligations set out in the OPMEP. Teams of PAJE accreditors visit each War College and assess the school and its curriculum, and make recommendations for improvement.

Where JPME is concerned, two issues impede evaluating whether PME institutions are meeting the goals of Goldwater-Nichols. The accreditation teams are made up of faculty from other PME institutions. This is a problem because they have a vested interest in finding that "all is well," so that teams from other schools will report the same during reciprocal visits. (They would also be responsible for coming up with alternatives if things were not satisfactory, a thankless task few accreditors want.) The 130-plus-page OPMEP instructions are the educational equivalent of a checklist, including the described taxonomy of desired learning objectives, learning areas, requirements for faculty and student ratios, and other "guidelines," all of which perpetuate a "training" versus "education" approach. For the 2009 PAJE visit to the Naval War College, each department created a spreadsheet that matched session titles to learning objectives resulting in matrices larger than 50 × 25 for two of the three departments.[22] Boxes were checked, but that does not equate to "learning."

Second, PAJE teams are created *ad hoc* for each visit, so no single team is responsible for any implementation or follow-up. When they do examine a school, it is only for about a week. The teams are provided with reams of reading material in advance, detailing how the schools are meeting the hefty OPMEP requirements, but sometimes these materials have clearly not been read before arrival. One accreditor demanded to see some curricular information at a PAJE meeting, only to have his aide quietly point out that the book in front of him was open to the page providing the information he was asking for.[d]

Understandably, the PAJE committees spend their time primarily reviewing the numerical information that they can most easily verify, rather than trying to make qualitative judgments about the value of the education being provided to the students. But even quantitative

---

d He wanted to know why the Naval War College didn't cover the Korean War. His binder was open to that case study.

indicators can be misleading. Student–faculty ratios, for example, are an important marker, but they are often skewed because numerous administrative positions are carefully categorized as faculty, even if they involve little or no core curriculum teaching. In the end, the whirlwind PAJE week is part ceremony and part box-check. The team, in fact, spends a good part of its time writing the draft of their final report on site, so that the expected good news can be delivered on the last day of their visit. Institutions found to have egregious violations in one area or another – a rarity – are given time to get their program to an acceptable level – a do-over.

On the civilian side, the degree programs at the War Colleges are reviewed by the same regional bodies that accredit other colleges and universities in the area, such as the New England Association of Schools and Colleges and its counterparts. The civilian academic overseers responsible for reviewing the degree programs every ten years perform much the same way as the PAJE teams. They are provided with similar stacks of glossy binders. They then arrive and march through the checklists and points of administrative process, consider such items as the administrative organization chart, the impact of having a new president every few years, and whether or not there is a faculty handbook and senate.

These and other issues would be important at civilian schools (where faculty have a voice in institutional policies) but are mostly irrelevant in an environment with contracted, rather than tenured, faculty. Moreover, civilian accreditors are unfamiliar with the vernacular and abbreviations of War Colleges – Joint Operations, PAJE, OPMEP, JPME – making analysis difficult, and are understandably dazzled by the efficiency of the military, given the general disorganization of civilian colleges. Like their PAJE counterparts, they too are happy to sign off on a tacitly predetermined final product.

Accreditation of civilian academic institutions has recently been coming under renewed scrutiny. A 2010 study titled *The Inmates Running the Asylum: An Analysis of Higher Education Accreditation*,[23] states that accreditation has evolved from a process intended to help institutions improve to one of checklist compliance of quantitative standards. For civilian academic institutions, accreditation is important to be eligible for federal loans and funding, irrelevant to PME. Thus although originally a voluntary process for civilian schools, accreditors are now gatekeepers. "Many institutions," the authors write, "believed that despite providing a high-quality education to their students, they were denied voluntary accreditation because, on paper, they did not measure up to quantitative standards."[24] The civilian accreditation process has become increasingly less transparent over the years as well.

Still, accreditation is an important quality control for both PME and civilian schools. Unfortunate as it is to say, the existence of these valuable Master's degree programs at the War Colleges has spawned repeated – and continuing – complaints from senior military leadership and DOD bureaucrats that graduate degrees are merely "gold plating" to JPME requirements. Senior DOD leaders believe the urban legend that additional curricular material was added to the JPME requirements only to satisfy the academic accreditors. This is patently false, but is a common canard by bureaucrats or military officers who want to cut costs, shorten, simplify, or eliminate PME programs. In the case of the Naval War College, the first PME school to be accredited, the courses as they stood were presented to academic accreditors, who agreed that they were degree-worthy, and accredited the program in 1984.[25] Whatever issues there may be with the academic programs or the accrediting process, nothing was ever added or changed to the JPME curriculum to meet those standards.[26] But, many DOD proposals (like shortening the Naval War College program to 90 days, an idea that was once seriously considered) would lose accreditation.

In fairness to both accreditation groups, they come with a checklist for review, and they follow it. They do not have the time, or the mandate, to look into substantive issues. How the institution defines education, why the faculty are not involved in the educational process at higher levels, the existence of questionable personnel practices, or whether the students have backgrounds that could get them through the rigorous admission processes and courses in programs like the Fletcher School or the Johns Hopkins School of Advanced International Studies (that the War Colleges generally consider to be their peer institutions) are all beyond their scope. They do their job as best they can, and leave.

Congress and the individual services also have roles in PME oversight. Congressman Ike Skelton championed and closely followed PME issues for many years, though since he lost his seat in 2010[27] nobody else has taken it up as a continued personal cause. Members of Congress with PME institutions in their districts are rightfully protective of them, similar to protecting NASA centers or any military base, as they can be among the largest employers in a district or state.

Occasional hearings are held,[28] but Congress these days understandably has bigger fish to fry than what goes on at War Colleges; and PME is a bargain (especially at the Naval War College) in terms of price per student for the specialized curricula taught. Whether or not that is recognized by Congress is another question.

Service interest in the War Colleges varies, and with varied impact. Close attention from the services is a mixed blessing. The negative effects of the Air Staff "help" with curriculum development given to the Air War College have already been described. Regarding the Army War College, as one of their faculty members once wryly put it, "The good news is that the Army loves its War College. The bad news is that the Army *really* loves its War College."[29] The Navy, on the other hand, as a traditionally deployed service, is more like a distant parent. That approach has yielded a stronger academic program, which the other services tend to appreciate more than the Navy itself.

Non-resident (distance) programs

Because the resident programs cannot handle the volume of officer education required in the 21st century, and because the services in many instances will not release officers from operational duty, non-resident, distance education programs have expanded significantly in recent years, as they have in civilian schools. Non-resident PME courses have become an expanding fiefdom within the PME world[30] because their numbers are significantly larger than those of the resident program. That means a big budget and consequent institutional clout.

To accommodate different circumstances, the distance version of the non-resident courses are packaged in several different ways. By legislation, the content is supposed to be "significantly derived" from the resident course – the mothership. PME distance education programs therefore cannot exist without the resident programs. Options for distance education range from programs on CD-ROMs that can travel anywhere (under the icecaps or to a war zone, for example) and do not require an (immediate) internet connection, to sophisticated online programs and in-person seminars that attempt to replicate the resident programs to as high a degree as possible. Students enrolled in these programs complete their coursework in addition to their often already more-than-full-time jobs.

Distance programs anywhere are a challenge. All the faculty and execution issues found in the PME resident programs are also found in the distance programs, and are often exacerbated. At the Naval War College, the resident department chairs theoretically have joint authority over hiring and evaluation of College of Distance Education (CDE) faculty in Newport and across the country. In practice, however, that policy is rarely adhered to, especially regarding hiring. Faculty are sometimes hired at an inflated faculty rank, sometimes with little regard to qualifications. While there are some excellent CDE instructors, some must be provided with very specific instructions and a prepared set of PowerPoint slides to teach each session, as their subject matter depth can be minimal.

For a time after Goldwater-Nichols was passed, it was possible (and relatively easy) for military officers to get "waivers" from JPME obligations if they were needed for operational duty. While all services took advantage of that option to some degree; the Navy, with its propensity for prioritizing sea duty and technical degrees[31] used it most of all. A decade ago, however, the ease of obtaining those waivers ceased. Consequently, distance programs became the only way for a large backlog of military officers to meet their JPME requirements so they would be eligible for promotion and joint positions.

What ensued was a race to the bottom in terms of which service could develop the non-resident JPME program that students could complete most quickly and with the least amount of effort. These individuals are, after all, completing these courses in addition to carrying out their full-time jobs. (Navy students report that their superiors and promotion boards often favorably view piling even more into their already busy days rather than taking a resident program away from the fleet.) The Air Force handily won the "quickest-easiest course" distance education program race. Students – from all services – were signing up as quickly as the Air Force could process them as, reportedly, the course exams were multiple choice, and a student could retake them as many times as necessary to figure out the answers and pass.

The military services are especially anxious to get these non-resident programs approved by the PAJE process and accredited, as this is where the services get the most academic box-checking accomplished. During my tenure as chair, there was particular pressure to attest to the academic integrity of new CDE programs, including the one to be delivered on CD-ROMs, despite concerns from all three teaching departments. In a 2003 memo from an active-duty Marine colonel serving as a departmental representative to a PAJE committee, the colonel noted that one of the PAJE members "sidelined" him and complained that she was being "stiff-armed" on departmental support for that new program.

Still, perhaps one of the greatest services of PME distance programs is the education in security studies it affords to government officials. The Naval War College has operated a "Fleet Seminar Program" for many years, including Washington, D.C. locations such as Capitol Hill and the Navy Yard. An instructor meets with the students in a night seminar program, replicating the Newport experience as closely as possible. That program is open to, and heavily subscribed to by, Congressional staff, toward attaining a Master's degree in security studies. Monitoring one of those Washington courses as chair, I ran into a former Air War College student, and graduate, who was taking the course for, as she said, "substance." Based on that and a slew of other testimonials, I would argue that the Navy's D.C. distance program is one of the best offered in PME, and should be the model for similar JPME programs. Whether they are truly graduate courses aimed primarily at education rather than training, however, remains a different question.

6 Recommendations and conclusion

> While I fully concur with your recommendations for transforming PME, I believe it would take another George Marshall and the full backing of the service secretaries and president ... There have been calls for reform before and little has been done. A profound pity.
>
> Wayne A. Silkett, Lieutenant Colonel, US Army (retired), former Army War College faculty member[1]

At an April 2012 panel on Professional Military Education in Washington, D.C., defense analyst Tom Ricks expressed apprehension that uncertainties about the rigor and value of PME would make it vulnerable to budget cuts. Specifically, he stated:

> I suspect that in the coming decade, any institution, department, or individual that cannot demonstrate a clear, positive contribution is going to get axed. My concern is that the baby will be thrown out with the bathwater. There is a lot of good in military education, but if you let the bad persist, it will drag down the rest.[2]

Senior Professional Military Education at the War Colleges is the primary opportunity afforded most of America's military leaders to expand their education and move from being the best and brightest in tactical and military operations, to joining their civilian peers at the strategic level of decision-making. It is too important to be sacrificed on the altar of inertia and bureaucratic and organizational politics. But that assumes Congress still feels it is important that as military officers advance in their careers they become more broadly educated, beyond their operational specialties. They must also understand and address strategic issues as the future advisors to civilian authorities. If that assumption is correct, then realities demand that the War Colleges rethink their educational responsibilities.

Not all officers who attend War Colleges will eventually be in strategic positions. I would argue, however, that even those who will never sit at a conference table making strategic decisions may well sit along the back row of the room, behind the decision-makers. They will only be able to assist their bosses if they understand the problems being addressed. Perhaps even more important, by virtue of their increasing diverse overseas missions, American military personnel are unofficially joining the ranks of America's diplomats in great numbers, and at more junior levels. Whether in war zones or in security cooperation assignments, the more prepared officers are to understand the complex aspects of their working environment, the more successful they will be. The globalized nature of the security environment and complex relations between nations likely to prevail in the future require a broad, strategic education for senior military officers.

So where should officers be educated? General Petraeus attended Princeton University and it served him well. But Princeton and its peers will never teach the required and highly specialized material available only in a War College. It is not their mission, and they would not do it well: university graduate schools are largely focussed on preparing graduate students to expand on theoretical issues within disciplines, rather than tackle policy issues. Furthermore, there is not nearly enough room at the nation's elite universities – which currently only take a handful of military students and cannot take many more – for the *thousands* of officers who must, and *should*, pass through the PME system each year.

Many in the military leadership would prefer to close the War Colleges and instead insert officers into even more engineering programs, and to become even more technocratic. Worse, officers may end up in mediocre social science programs, taking irrelevant courses, just to check the required "education" box on military fitness reports. Alternatively, officers might all also be told to simply enroll in online academic programs. That would be the clearest signal of all that education is not really valued by military leadership, and would begin the race to find the easiest, fastest way to meet the box-check requirement.

It is worth repeating that when the best and the brightest of military students choose a War College education over a Princeton education, the War Colleges will have achieved success. That is a high bar. But

Princeton and other programs at places like SAIS, Fletcher, the Kennedy School, and elsewhere have made an effort to draw from the best of the War Colleges by including courses in grand strategy and national security in their curricula, and are succeeding. The War Colleges should, similarly, take the best of what happens in academia – critical thinking, challenging students, and knowledge taught and generated by well-educated faculty – and help officers to apply all of this to complex problems. The War Colleges cannot be Princeton, nor should they. But perhaps they can and should be a bit more like Princeton and a bit less like a training exercise.

My recommendations will be addressed in the same categories in which they were considered in previous chapters. I will also include a category of *institutional* recommendations, to include points that are foundational or cross between other categories. These recommendations are by no means exhaustive, nor intended to convey a complete solution. They are offered as part of what I hope will be an extended discussion of how to improve the quality of education at the War Colleges – a goal I consider important, even crucial, to the Nation's future national security.

My first recommendation is that a study be conducted by an *independent group*, not a DOD contractor, and not comprised of individuals with a vested interest in the outcome – such as former War College administrators. This study should gather accurate information and data on points that I have been able to gather only through anecdotal evidence. This book has relied on my own records and what others have been willing to share, as well as open-source and self-reported data. While I am grateful to the numerous individuals who have provided their own insights, information, and opinions, more data are needed, and they need to be gathered by an organization or group with the authority to ask probing questions and get full and non-distorted answers.

Questions might include: Who actually makes up War College faculties? What percentage of institutional resources is spent on the core JPME educational mission at War Colleges, versus other missions? At what rate have administrative positions grown at the War Colleges? How are PME positions competed? How are academic ranks given or earned? What role should practitioners play in PME? How do the scholarly activities of War College faculties compare with the institutions that the War Colleges consider their peer programs? There are a host of other pertinent questions well worth asking as well.

Such a study, or studies, must be independent because self-reported information is too easily skewed or favorably packaged. Sometimes, as well, self-studies omit important information not specifically asked for by those unfamiliar with the issues or institution. Data gathered by DOD contractors is often plagued by similar issues because the contractors want to please the client. A study by an independent, congressionally appointed panel, or the General Accounting Office, would be appropriate.

Undoubtedly, there will be those who disagree with some or many of the assertions made in this book about personnel, administrative management, student matriculation, the curriculum – and everything else. Even with accurate data to draw from, there will be disagreements about best practices and goals, but data would provide a good place from which an authoritative, analytic follow-on discussion might commence. An area about which data will be especially difficult to gather, though, will be institutional culture, and that, again, is the heart of the matter.

Culture

Culture cannot be fixed by dictum. Cultural changes occur based on the actions of leadership about expectations of the organization and its people. Megan McArdle paraphrased an old joke in an article examining the dysfunctional cultural of some American companies: "How many experts does it take to turn around a big company? Only one – but the company has to really want to change."[3] Therefore, if the military recognizes and supports the need for a broadly educated senior officer corps, as public rhetoric of top military leaders would lead the public and Congress to believe, then action must more closely align with that rhetoric. Officers at the O-5 and O-6 level (lieutenant colonels and colonels in the Army, Air Force and Marines, and commanders and captains in the Navy) do not need more technical training. As they become more senior, they will be leaving the flying, ship-driving and tank-driving (the fun jobs, as some see them) to younger officers. The higher one advances in a military career, or any career, the broader the education they need, and that goal needs to be reinforced by the chain of command.

In practice, this means that all services must make a commitment to education that is reflected in selection for War College resident programs, and in promotions. Workers only put effort into those activities their employer rewards, and so box-check activities are given the attention they deserve – minimal. For all the services, this will mean seriously building time into an officer's career for education and not just a last stop prior to retirement.

Next, an assignment to a War College as a faculty member should be at least as competitive for a military officer as for a student. While a War College faculty assignment might well be appropriate as a "twilight tour" for military officers who can share their career-long experience, a fair number of PME instructors should also still have active careers. If a War College is important, then a significant percentage of the military faculty should be promotable and a War College assignment should be viewed as a prestigious addition to their fitness reports.

Finally, the military services must demand a rigorous educational program that will allow individuals *to fail courses without ruining their careers*. One suggestion has been to simply do away with grades at the War Colleges, because there are some military officers "who might not excel in a formal educational milieu who are nonetheless consummate military professionals."[4] While perhaps true (is it unreasonable to expect that senior military leaders should be able to pass a reasonably rigorous graduate program?), that they are all being perfunctorily passed and awarded degrees is what is currently subjecting the program to skepticism. Doing away with grades and still passing them all through would do nothing to alleviate that problem; in fact it would make it worse. Further, accreditation would be put at risk, if not outright revoked. If that happened, the students would undoubtedly revert to past ways, when they attended War College knowing they would all pass, consequently paid minimal attention to the curriculum, and instead enrolled in and focussed on a local graduate night school program to get a Master's degree valuable post-retirement.

Differentiating the standards for completing JPME from those required for a Master's degree at the War Colleges seems the better approach toward increasing rigor and hence program credibility. Far more students will pass the JPME requirement necessary to advance in their career, while the Master's degree would be conferred to those who had truly demonstrated superior academic performance, allowing a more normal bell curve of success and failure. This would force students to be more serious about their studies, because they all recognize the value of the Master's degree in retirement (and for some, in their military career, for promotion). At the least, the tacit institutional mandate that everyone must pass should end. The War Colleges must be more serious educational institutions, and so the institutions must take themselves more seriously academically.

I am not underestimating the institutional challenges. Judith Hicks Stiehm wrote in her concluding chapter about the Army War College in 2002:

> A crucial change would involve faculty capacities and functions. Efforts to hire more Ph.D.s and more civilian faculty have not changed much. Hiring retired officers who have earned a Ph.D. while on active duty does not raise the standards or open the atmosphere. More faculty need to be engaged in the profession. They need to do research that is submitted to peer review and to design courses that create "discomfort.[5]

It is a testimony to the power of inertia and the commitment to the status quo within PME generally that I am now repeating many of those same recommendations in 2012.

Institutional

When considering how to make the War Colleges more effective educational institutions, it should be remembered, first and foremost, that the job of the War Colleges is to educate students and make them better defenders of the United States of America and its interests and allies around the world. Other missions are secondary, even potentially distractive. Therefore, institutional mission priority, with all the affiliated time and resource commitments, should be given to educating the students to make them equals to the best of their civilian counterparts in the defense community, as Admiral Turner insisted 40 years ago. Otherwise, they will fail in their responsibility to provide the best strategic leadership for the military, and the best strategic advice to civilian leaders.

Academic freedom

Academic freedom should be a fundamental principle of each War College (and more generally, at all PME institutions) to assure that students are fearlessly challenged by the best minds the PME system can bring to bear, and that they feel free to respond to the challenges. As both faculty and students are government employees, there are inherent boundaries to academic freedom, but those are non-intrusive and easily manageable if those boundaries are made clear. Generally speaking, that means no use of classified material (obviously) and criticism should be focussed on policies rather than on individual people. (Frankly, most faculty prefer not to work with classified material. Even working on often highly classified space security issues, I do not work in the classified area and have never suffered professionally because of it.) Nor does focussing on criticizing policies rather than individual people inhibit professional work; I have been a critic of missile defense – and, obviously, of PME – as part of my professional work, keeping the focus on policies rather than specific individuals. In fact, some PME faculty members have regularly critiqued policies of various administrations, in articles and blogs,[6] as part of their contribution to the debate on national defense. PME should trust their faculty, because most them already understand their unique responsibility.

As chair, I had an instance where a faculty member personally criticized a member of the Rhode Island congressional delegation by name in print, and the Admiral received many concerned phone calls about that. He was rightly angry and the faculty member was reprimanded. But that happened only once in eight years, and was one op-ed among dozens, even hundreds, of books, articles, blogs, and presentations. The Naval War College should be the model here for other PME schools in its handling and support of academic freedom.

In return, PME faculty should also adhere to the same boundaries of academic freedom as other academics. The 1940 guidelines of the American Association of University Professors (AAUP) on academic freedom speak for themselves:

1   Teachers are entitled to full freedom in research and in the publication of the results, subject to the adequate performance of their other academic duties; but research for pecuniary return should be based upon an understanding with the authorities of the institution.

2   Teachers are entitled to freedom in the classroom in discussing their subject, but they should be careful not to introduce into their teaching controversial matter which has no relation to their subject. Limitations of academic freedom because of religious or other aims of the institution should be clearly stated in writing at the time of the appointment.

3   College and university teachers are citizens, members of a learned profession, and officers of an educational institution. When they speak or write as citizens, they should be free from institutional censorship or discipline, but their special position in the community imposes special obligations. As scholars and educational officers, they should remember that the public may judge their profession and their institution by their utterances. Hence they should at all times be accurate, should exercise appropriate restraint, should show respect for the opinions of others, and should make every effort to indicate that they are not speaking for the institution.[7]

Simply put, faculty should be protected in the freedom to represent their own professional views, as long as they keep in mind that they must not represent their institutions or disgrace themselves or their institution.

Indeed, faculty at civilian institutions should adhere to these guidelines as well. Harvard President Larry Summers apparently felt the limits were being stretched in 2002 when he chastised faculty member Cornel West for focussing too much on his rap CD and not enough on academics, as well as for leading a political committee supporting Reverend Al Sharpton in a possible campaign for the presidency.[8] West left Harvard for Princeton.

Overall, the War Colleges are likely *better than* their civilian counterparts in holding faculty accountable for *public* slanderous, sexist, racist, or similar remarks. What they need is greater freedom to offer substantive contributions to the national security debate.

Administrative bloat

In both civilian and PME institutions, focussing on the primary educational task of the institutions, and especially in times of fiscal austerity, requires that administrative staff positions be scrubbed based on necessity. Thinning the herd of administrators will allow more funding and attention to be put toward the educational mission. In PME, as in civilian schools, administrative bloat drives up costs per student. In civilian schools this results in tuition hikes. In PME, the taxpayer pays the bill.

Cutting administration will increase institutional efficiency as well. Administrators create layers of bureaucracy focussed on processes and paperwork, which, in turn, are often delegated to the faculty. (A military colleague referred to these positions as "tasking jobs" because the individuals holding them did little themselves; tasking duties to others instead.) These layers of administration also create distance between faculty and the school's leadership, as president and deans become more and more isolated. This is especially a problem when administrators have no academic experience on which to base their decisions, and see the faculty as staff whose job it is to meet administrative tasks rather than to teach and conduct research.

Fiscal responsibility

Fiscal austerity and integrity requires getting the most bang for the government buck wherever possible. Practices such as having two schools to teach JPME 1 and 2 should be reconsidered. The workload for faculty is significantly less with two faculties, thereby allowing more time for both curriculum development and scholarly activity that will allow faculty to remain current in their fields. But the costs and benefits of two schools and two faculties must be weighed against each other.

Likewise, the practice of assigning multiple faculty members into a classroom at the same time should be reviewed. Under the best of circumstances team teaching can have value, reducing workload for faculty so that individuals can focus their efforts, and increasing the perspectives and expertise to which the students are exposed. More often, however, too many faculty members in the classroom results in an under-utilization of teachers. The practice of team teaching is superfluous and an expensive waste of resources.

Finally, the cost of field trips should be reviewed. While they were not extensively considered as part of this work, generally, how much students get from either a day trip or two weeks in some far-off place, as in the case of the regional trips still taken at some War Colleges, seems appropriate for reconsideration. My own experience was that these trips are largely reposes from the classroom for the students; nobody becomes an expert on anything on a junket.

Students

Service leaders must tell students that their War College assignment is a year of intellectual challenge and rigor. Every effort will be made to ensure student success, but not everyone will leave with a Master's degree or high honors. PME performance expectations should be high. Detailers who feel their charges need some family time should suggest an assignment other than a demanding graduate program that accomplishes in a year what most top universities take twice as long to achieve.

Likewise, students should be told in no uncertain terms that they are not the masters or owners of the schools. They are not clients or peers. They should be made to realize the privilege of holding a graduate scholarship – for that is what it is – granted to them by the people of the United States to study for a year on full pay and with no other obligations. If they do not want or appreciate that opportunity, they should seek assignment elsewhere.

PME students, like their civilian counterparts, are fickle regarding what they want and how they want it. They are professionals in their own fields but, by and large, not in the fields addressed at the War College level. They can provide data points on curriculum relevance, but faculty should not be expected to chase student expectations like a cat chasing a laser pointer. Accordingly, student evaluations should not reign supreme in PME. But if students consistently rate a faculty member low on teaching evaluations, those should certainly be a consideration for continued employment.

More importantly, initial indications from the students that a faculty member is struggling should be used by their supervisor to provide the faculty member with remedial help, not as a club with which to threaten them. All faculty will at some point get a "seminar from hell", which for some reason doesn't gel, is angry at the world, or where there are simply personality clashes. But faculty should not be punished for occasional student dissatisfaction: students by their nature often resent being challenged. Sometimes, learning only occurs by making students angry enough to consider carefully and reflect on their own positions, perhaps for the first time. That is the job of the faculty.

Faculty

PME institutions need to create a better balance between civilian academics and military faculty. Active-duty military officers are crucial to the PME mission, and should be the first choice to teach the courses on operational warfare, rather than former officers far removed from today's force. The number of active-duty billets assigned to War Colleges is increasingly tight, and if officers are promotable or likely to get assignments beyond their War College tour, their recent operational and often command experience should be maximized. They do what civilians largely cannot, and should not be wasted as "deanlets" or teaching assistants. On the other hand, active-duty military are not needed in all departments. Unless they have a unique specialty in the subject, why is an active-duty military officer needed to teach history or international relations?

Hiring active-duty military officers immediately into civilian positions upon retirement should be reserved for exceptional officers who have demonstrated great future promise beyond their operational specialties. These individuals need not have a doctoral degree. There are other ways to demonstrate engagement in their fields, first by declaring what field it is that they see themselves developing and maintaining an expertise in. Faculty must be required to stay demonstrably active in a substantive field, to assure their ability to contribute to curriculum development. Annual evaluations can then be made regarding progress and achievement. Professional achievement, teaching proficiency (based on trends over time), and service ought to be the bases for retention for all faculty.

Regarding civilian faculty, tenure or a tenure-like system for civilians needs to be in place to force peer-reviewed productivity, prevent the accumulation of expensive academic "dead wood," and allow the senior faculty to speak truth to power without fear of retribution. Granting tenure on hire should be available to recruit top scholars, some of whom may be hired into leadership positions (especially those responsible for evaluating faculty) based on qualifications both for the position and for a full professor position at a peer institution.

Additionally, adherence to a faculty rank system based on merit and achievement will gain the War Colleges significant credibility among other academic institutions who need to be PME partners in national defense. This will help the War Colleges attract top talent to come to

PME. Moreover, PME departments should offer more visiting professorships, to attract people who want to learn about PME and who can contribute to academic debates over grand strategy. They need not be academics only: PME institutions should not want to have faculties that resemble those in the civilian world, which are often too theory-oriented. Again, balance is key.

While the commandant or president of a War College will and should be a general officer, faculty should have a role in War College administration. That is not to say that PME institutions necessarily need to have "faculty senates:" they can be hives of mischief and obstruction as civilian schools painfully know. But there is a considerable amount to be said for departmental collegiality, if only as a quality of life issue. Faculty should not be cowered into submission, fearful of their contract not being renewed if they voice opinions. Also, if faculty members are not constantly worrying about a next contract they will be more willing to innovate. A tenure system is a necessary but not sufficient step toward a more efficient and effective faculty. Additionally, faculty should have input into administrative (provosts, deans) and faculty hiring decisions much more than is currently the norm, which would engender a sense of buy-in and collegiality far more than a faculty senate or similar structure. And finally, *more career academics need to be included in PME decision-making roles.*

Curriculum

Faculty should be responsible for curriculum development. Accordingly, they should be held to account for the degree to which that curriculum is both of high scholarly quality and relevant to the issues of national security. PME cannot serve the narrow interests of political theorists, military historians, process-oriented practitioners, or retired military officers comfortable only with a narrow range of material. If education and intellectual agility are the goals, then educators at PME institutions must create a curriculum that forces students to get over their predilection for certainty and comfort, and for black-and-white issues with clear answers. The curriculum, and professors who teach it, must defeat this attitude, not play to it. The goal of temporary student happiness must be set aside. Military faculty and administrators in particular must resist the natural urge to be overly sympathetic and to want to mentor these younger versions of themselves, using training-friendly methods and approaches rather than rigorous education standards.

Conclusion

On 16 July 2012 General Martin Dempsey, Chairman of the Joint Chiefs of Staff, issued a Joint Education White Paper, which he also posted on Facebook for comment in addition to normal channels of dissemination.[9] In it he emphasized that the purpose of PME was to "develop leaders by conveying a broad body of professional knowledge and developing the habits of mind essential to our profession," including "intellectual curiosity, coupled with openness to new ideas." Dempsey, aware that the students do not attain this on their own, also discusses faculty needs: "The quality of professors and teachers has been and will remain an enduring and essential component in our institutional commitment to joint education" and so PME should seek to "attract and maintain civilian and military faculty who are among the very best and brightest of their contemporaries." I could not agree more: the goals of the Chief's White Paper are much the same goals as I have sought in presenting this book. His direction is clear; we can only hope that the PME system will follow it.

With the United States currently engaged in military actions around the world, a "War College" should be exactly that: both a college and a serious preparation for the defense of the nation. As Stephen Luce described Newport, it should be "a place of original research on all questions relating to war and statesmanship connected with war, or the prevention of war."[10] That means a year of hard and necessary study, and not primarily a continued exercise in building student self-esteem. That was one of the goals of the Goldwater-Nichols reforms, and it is within reach if we are willing to recommit to the vision put forward over 25 years ago.

Notes

1 Why War Colleges?

1 This book builds on work published earlier. See: "Teach Tough, Think Tough: Why Military Education Must Change," *AOL Defense*, 15 June 2011, http://defense.aol.com/2011/06/15/teach-tough-think-tough/ (accessed 26 March 2012); "Teach Tough, Think Tough: Three Ways to Fix the War Colleges," *AOL Defense*, 23 July 2011 http://defense.aol.com/2011/07/23/teach-tough-think-tough-three-ways-to-fix-the-war-colleges/ (accessed 26 March 2012); "A comment on Does Keeping PME Relevant Mean Fixing Faculty First?", UNSI blog, 23 August 2011, http://blog.usni.org/2011/08/23/guest-post-a-comment-on-%E2%80%9Cdoes-keeping-pme-relevant-mean-fixing-faculty-first%E2%80%9D-by-dr-joan-johnson-freese/ (accessed 26 March 2012); "The Reform of Military Education: Twenty Five Years Later," *Orbis*, Winter 2012, 135–152. *Orbis* is the quarterly journal of the Foreign Policy Research Institute (FPRI) in Philadelphia.

2 Admiral James Stavridis, "Read...Think...and Write," 15 August 2011, http://www.aco.nato.int/saceur/read-think-write.aspx (accessed 26 March 2012).

3 Admiral James Stavridis, "Read...Think...and Write," 15 August 2011. http://www.aco.nato.int/saceur/read-think-write.aspx (accessed 26 March 2012).

4 Detailed budget information for PME institutions can be difficult to obtain and decipher. In FY 2008, the Navy allocated $2.1 billion for training and education, though not all of that was for the War College. United States Navy, "Department of the Navy's Fiscal Year 2008 President's Budget," Fiscal Year 2008/2009 Department of the Navy Budget Materials, Assistant Secretary of the Navy for Financial Management and Comptroller, 5 February 2007, http://www.finance.hq.navy.mil/FMB/08PRES/HIGHBOOK/08PRESs_Brief.pdf (accessed 26 March 2012). According to a May 2009 Self-study (for the CJCS PAJE Team, for JPME Phase 2) for Fiscal Year 2009, the Naval War College "has been funded with $62.8M of directly allocated O&M,N funds and $4.1M of RDT&E funds. The college is programmed to receive an additional $4.6M from international IOCE funds; another $0.892M for

International Monetary Education and Training and $0.9M is budgeted for the Field Studies Program at the College" (p. 11).

5   For a catalog of PME institutions, including those beyond War Colleges, see Cynthia A. Watson, *Military Education: A Reference Handbook,* Praeger, 2007.

6   Officer Professional Military Education Policy, CJCSI 1800.01D, 15 July 2009. Appendix A, Annex A., http://www.dtic.mil/cjcs_directives/cdata/unlimit/1800_01.pdf (accessed 4 April 2012).

7   After the failed Iranian hostage rescue attempt, two important articles appeared in *Armed Forces Journal International* advocating defense reorganization and paving the way for Goldwater-Nichols, one by General David C. Jones, "Why the Joint Chiefs of Staff Must Change," March 1982, and then Army Chief of Staff General Edward C. Meyer, "The JCS: How Much Reform is Needed?" March 1982.

8   Watson, 2007, p. 14.

9   See: William M. Steele and Robert Kupiszewski, "Joint Education: Where do We Go from Here?" *Joint Forces Quarterly,* Winter 1993–94, pp. 63–70.

10   United States House of Representatives, Subcommittee of the Committee on Armed Services, "Another Crossroads? Professional Military Education Twenty Years after the Goldwater-Nichols Act and the Skeleton Panel," HASC publication No. 111-67, 20 May, 2009. The quote about "fighting done by fools" is widely misattributed to Thucydides (as it is in the HASC report) but was actually penned by W.F. Butler in 1889.

11   "Challenge! A New Approach to a Professional Education at the Naval War College," *Naval War College Review,* November–December 1972, p.3.

12   Ibid.

13   Mackubin Thomas Owens, "Lessons Learned," National Review Online, 7 August 2006, http://www.nationalreview.com/nrd/article/?q=NDk3Ym EwN2Y5OTg4NTZmNzhjOTdmYTRjYzEyNGFjY2M= (accessed 26 March 2012).

14   "The Naval War College in Transition," *Naval War College Review,* Centennial Issue 1884–1984, September–October 1984, p. 8.

15   Samuel Huntington, *The Soldier and the State: The Theory and Politics of Civil–Military Relations,* Belknap Press, 1981. Drawing an example from the American approach to antisubmarine warfare in 1942, Eliot Cohen and John Gooch provide an example in their 1991 book *Military Misfortunes: The Anatomy of Failure in War*: "In a nutshell, the Navy's leadership defined its problem as that of acquiring technical information, not assimilating new forms of organization." Anchor Books, pp. 87–88.

16   Mackubin Thomas Owens, "Lessons Learned," *National Review Online,* 7 August 2006, http://www.nationalreview.com/nrd/article/?q=NDk3Ym EwN2Y5OTg4NTZmNzhjOTdmYTRjYzEyNGFjY2M= (accessed 26 March 2012).

17   Stephen Hadley and William Perry (co-chairs), The QDR in Perspective: Meeting America's National Security Needs in the 21st Century – The Final Report of the Quadrennial Defense Review Independent Panel (Washington,

D.C.: United States Institute of Peace, 2010), http://www.usip.org/quadrennial-defense-review-independent-panel/view-the-report; Scott Bethel, Aaron Prupas, Tomisalv Ruby and Michael Smith, "Developing Air Force Strategists: Change Culture, Reverse Careerism," *Joint Forces Quarterly*, 58, 3 (2010): 82–88.

18 Barry Watts, Center for Strategic and Budgetary Assessment, "U.S. Combat Training, Operational Art and Strategic Competence: Problems and Opportunities," 2008, http://www.csbaonline.org/wp-content/uploads/2011/02/2008.08.21-Combat-Training-Operational-Art-Strategic-Competence.pdf (accessed 26 March 2012).

19 Ft. #1 in Scott Bethel, Aaron Prupas, Tomisalv Ruby and Michael Smith, "Developing Air Force Strategists: Change Culture, Reverse Careerism," *Joint Forces Quarterly*, 58, 3 (2010); Gregory D. Foster, "Research, Writing and the Mind of the Strategist," *Joint Forces Quarterly*, 11, (1996), 111–115.

20 Scott Bethel, Aaron Prupas, Tomisalv Ruby and Michael Smith, "Developing Air Force Strategists: Change Culture, Reverse Careerism," *Joint Forces Quarterly*, 58, 3 (2010), 82–88.

21 *Another Crossroads*, p. vii.

22 *Another Crossroads*. These points and the theme of "fighting the last war" and failure to transform educational programs and approaches for a post-Cold War world are addressed throughout the Preface and the Executive Summary.

23 *Another Crossroads*, p.107, citing Jeffrey D. McCausland and Neil Weissman, Educating Leaders in an Age of Uncertainty – The Future of Military War Colleges: A Research Study for the Smith Richardson Foundation, Dickinson College Leadership in Conflict Initiative, Carlisle, Pennsylvania, 15 December 2005, p. 347.

24 George E. Reed, "What's Wrong and What's Right with the War Colleges," *DefensePolicy.Org*, online, 1 July 2011, http://www.defensepolicy.org/2011/george-reed/what%E2%80%99s-wrong-and-right-with-the-war-colleges (accessed 26 March 2012).

25 Daniel Hughes, "Professors in the Colonels' World," in Douglas Higbee (ed.), *Military Culture and Education* (Burlington, VT: Ashgate, 2010).

26 Howard Wiarda, *Military Brass versus Civilian Academics at the National War College: Clash of Cultures* (Lanham, MD: Lexington Books, 2011).

27 Mackubin Thomas Owens, "Lessons Learned," *National Review Online*, 7 August 2006.

28 Robert H. Scales, "Too Busy to Learn?" *Proceedings*, February 2010.

29 Judith Hicks Stiehm, *The U.S. Army War College: Military Education in a Democracy* (Philadelphia, PA: Temple University Press, 2002).

30 Charles Allen, "Redress of Military Education: The Clarion Call," *Joint Forces Quarterly*, Fall 2010.

31 Tom Ricks, "Need Budget Cuts? We Probably Can Start by Shutting Down the Air War College," *The Best Defense*, 11 April 2011, http://ricks.foreignpolicy.com/posts/2011/04/11/need_budget_cuts_we_probably_can_start_by_shutting_the_air_war_college (accessed 26 March 2012).

32   Stiehm, pp. 182–187.

33   Stiehm, p. 183.

34   19 April 2009.

35   Farrar, Straus & Giroux, 2007.

36   Bruce Flemming, *Annapolis Autumn: Life, Death and Literature at the U.S. Naval Academy*, The New Press, 2005.

37   Tom Ricks, "Need Budget Cuts? We Probably Can Start by Shutting the Air War College," *The Best Defense*, 11 April 2011, http://ricks.foreignpolicy.com/posts/2011/04/11/need_budget_cuts_we_probably_can_start_by_shutting_the_air_war_college (accessed 11 May 2012).

38   David H. Petraeus, "Beyond the Cloister," *The American Interest*, July–August 2007, http://www.the-american-interest.com/article.cfm?piece=290 (accessed 26 March 2012).

39   Reed, 2011, p. 3.

40   Ralph Peters, "Learning to Lose," *The American Interest*, July–August 2007, http://www.the-american-interest.com/article.cfm?piece=291 (accessed 26 March 2012).

41   30 August 2009, http://media.washingtonpost.com/wp-srv/politics/documents/Assessment_Redacted_092109.pdf (accessed 26 March 2012).

42   Michael Hastings, "The Runaway General," *Rolling Stone,* 22 June 2010, http://www.rollingstone.com/politics/news/the-runaway-general-20100622 (accessed 26 March 2012).

43   Taylor Trade Publishing, 2011.

44   Cynthia Watson, in Gabriel Marcella (ed.) *Teaching Strategy: Challenge and Response,* (Carlisle, PA: Strategic Studies Institute, 2010).

45   Watson, 2010, p. 150.

46   Watson, 2010, p. 173.

47   20 May 2010.

48   Peter Schmidt, "Investigators Say Naval Academy Punished Professor Who Criticized Affirmative Action," *Chronicle of Higher Education*, 26 January 2011, http://chronicle.com/article/Investigators-Say-Naval/126064/ (accessed 26 March 2012)

49   Dulles, VA: Potomac Books, 2010.

50   Peter Feaver, United States Naval Institute, *Proceedings* (April 2011), pp. 75–76.

51   Tom Ricks, "Fiasco at the Army War College," *The Best Defense*, 7 January 2009, http://ricks.foreignpolicy.com/posts/2009/01/07/fiasco_at_the_army_war_college (accessed 26 March 2012)

52   Naval War College professor Don Chisholm, quoted in "Does Keeping PME Relevant Mean Fixing the Faculty First?" USNI blog, 14 August 2011.

53   Todd Harrison, Analysis of the FY 2012 Defense Budget, Center for Strategic and Budgetary Analysis, p. 29.

2 Warriors and scholars

1   The military is not alone in, wrongly, using training and education as synonymous. Rosa Brooks, a fellow at the New America Foundation and Professor at Georgetown Law School wrote about the deficiencies of government officials in the development of grand strategy in 2012: "This is an area where the United States does shamefully badly. Most executive-branch agencies offer staff (junior or senior) little if any meaningful training in management, strategic planning, or policy implementation... But if talented people are untrained, they can still end up doing a lot of dumb things... This isn't rocket science; it's mostly pretty basic stuff. Get 30 senior officials together, and ask them to list 'Things I know now, and wish I'd known earlier.' The training curriculum for federal officials will pretty much write itself." "Obama Needs a Grand Strategy," *Foreign Policy Online,* 23 January 2012, http://www.foreignpolicy.com/articles/2012/01/23/obama_needs_a_grand_strategy (accessed 26 March 2012).

2   The Naval Academy has not escaped the push for (favorable) metrics either. Part of Bruce Fleming's exposé on admissions practices at Annapolis has focussed on inflated metrics. He questioned the Academy's stated admission rate of 7.5%, one of the highest in the country and a key measure of selectivity of the students. After obtaining data through the Freedom of Information Act, the rate was found to be closer to 50%, inaccurately measured by the institution for the lower rate by including incomplete applications. See Daniel de Vise's reports on Bruce Fleming's guest post in "Naval Academy Professor: A Veneer of Selectivity," *The Washington Post,* 30 December 2011.

3   John Hattendorf *et al., Sailors and Scholars: The Centennial History of the U.S. Naval War College* (Newport, RI, Naval War College Press, 1984), pp. 27–28.

4   Reed, p. 3.

5   A bit ironically, and illustrating that being dismissive of civilian professionals' advice extends beyond PME, that admiral went on to head the naval historical command, responsible for the safekeeping of the Navy's valuable treasures. The command came under investigation after the admiral decided the command was "too introverted and academic" and that he wanted more "forward-looking historians." Consequently, he turned away from the advice of the largely civilian professionals who worked for him with the result that, according to the investigation report, "the history and heritage of the United States Navy is in jeopardy." Also cited as part of the command problem was "a major growth in upper levels of management which insulate him from the professionals he employs," much as is the case with commandants and presidents in PME. See Sam Fellman, "IG Report Says Naval History 'In Jeopardy,'" *Navy Times,* 8 January 2012, http://www.navytimes.com/news/2012/01/navy-history-critical-inspector-general-report-010812w/ (accessed 26 March 2012).

6   Rebecca L. Frerichs and Stephen R. DiRienzo, "Establishing a Framework for Intelligence Education and Training", *Joint Forces Quarterly,* 62, (2011), 70–71.

7   See: Megan McArdle, "Why Companies Fail," *The Atlantic,* March 2012, pp. 28–32.

8   Wiarda, pp. 70–75.

9   Commander Jorge Garcia, "A Leadership Problem," */luce.nt/*, p. 36, http://www.usnwc.edu/Lucent/OpenPdf.aspx?id=103&Title=Evolution (accessed 26 March 2012).

10   Malcolm Gladwell, "Cocksure," *The New Yorker*, 27 July 2009.

11   Wyatt Olsen, "Do Fired Navy COs Suffer from 'Bathsheba Syndrome'?" *Stars and Stripes*, 14 March 2012, http://www.stripes.com/news/navy/do-fired-navy-cos-suffer-from-bathsheba-syndrome-1.171525

12   Dean Ludwig and C. Longenecker, "The Bathsheba Syndrome: The Ethical Failure of Successful Leaders," *Journal of Business Ethics,* 12, 77–85.

13   Manan Ahmed, *The National*, 4 March 2011, http://www.thenational.ae/arts-culture/books/flying-blind-us-foreign-policys-lack-of-expertise (accessed 26 March 2012).

14   Manan Ahmed, *The National*, 4 March 2011.

15   For another commentary on academic culture see Ronald J. Granieri's blog post at *The Recovering Politician*, "A Glimpse Behind the Ivy Curtain," 16 July 2012, http://therecoveringpolitician.com/friends/ronaldg/ronald-j-granieri-a-glimpse-behind-the-ivy-curtain (accessed 4 August 2012).

16   Studies are increasingly refuting the idea that unless individuals are held to strict office hours they will slack off. In fact, some companies allowing individuals to work their own schedules are seeing increased productivity. Lydia Dishman, "Unlimited Vacation Doesn't Create Clackers – It Ensures Productivity," *Fast Company,* 9 March 2012, http://www.fastcompany.com/ 1823415/why-unlimited-vacation-policies-ensure-productivity (accessed 26 March 2012).

17   Stephen M. Walt, "International Affairs and the Public Sphere," *Transformations of the Public Sphere*, Social Science Research Council, http://publicsphere.ssrc.org/walt-international-affairs-and-the-public-sphere/ (accessed 26 March 2012).

18   Walt, footnote 1: See David Newsom, "Foreign Policy and Academia,*"* *Foreign Policy* 101 (1995-96); and Alexander L. George, "Foreword," in Miroslav Nincic and Joseph Lepgold (eds.) *Being Useful: Policy Relevance and International Relations Theory* (Ann Arbor, MI: University of Michigan Press, 2000). This sense of dissatisfaction is not a new phenomenon. Nearly 60 years ago, Hans J. Morgenthau complained that "the retreat into the trivial, the formal, the methodological, the purely theoretical, the remotely historical – in short, the politically irrelevant – is the unmistakable sign of a 'non-controversial' political science that has neither friends nor enemies because it has no relevance for the great political issues in which society has a stake." See M. Benjamin Mollov, *Power and Transcendance: Hans J. Morgenthau and the Jewish Experience* (Lexington, KY: Lexington Books, 2002), p. 42.

19   Walt, footnote 2: Lawrence Mead, "Scholasticism in Political Science," *Perspectives on Politics*, 8, 2 (June 2010).

20   Matt Westmoreland, "Tenure Rough Road for Professors," *The Daily Princetonian*, 16 May 2008, http://www.dailyprincetonian.com/2008/0http://publicsphere.ssrc.org/walt-international-affairs-and-the-public-sphere/5/16/21215/ (accessed 26 March 2012).

21 Steven Wright, "History Dept. Receives Critical External Review," *The Chronicle*, 10 October 2000, http://dukechronicle.com/article/history-dept-receives-critical-external-review (accessed 26 March 2012).

22 See, for example, poll data on the political leanings on academics and military officers, http://abcnews.go.com/blogs/politics/2008/07/taking-aim-at-t/ (accessed 27 March 2012); http://www.insidehighered.com/news/2007/10/08/politics (accessed 27 March 2012).

23 March 2006.

24 Christopher P. Cavas, "Deputy CNO Sestak 'Reassigned': New CNO Reportedly Makes Move Due to 'Poor Command Climate'," *Navy Times*, 25 July 2005, http://www.navytimes.com/legacy/new/1-292925-995180.php (accessed 27 March 2012).

25 Operational commands are pressured to show "all as well" in technical fields also, as evidence by a cheating scandal aboard the nuclear submarine *USS Memphis*. According to press reports, "sailors know how to handle the nuclear technology, but commanders competing with one another to show proficiency have made tests so difficult – and so detached from the sailors' actually need – that crew members sometimes bend the rules." Michael Melia, "Navy Submarine *USS Memphis* Hit by Exam Cheating Scandal," *Huffington Post*, 15 August 2011.

26 Writing about PME while on the faculty at the Command and Staff College of Marine Corps University, Janeen Klinger stated a very different view in 2004. "Most surprisingly, given the fact that any military organization tends to be male-dominated, is that the environment is not inhospitable to women, although the expectation is that it might be a barrier to recruitment." "Academics and Professional Military Education," *Academic Exchange Quarterly*, Summer 2004, 8, 2, http://www.higher-ed.org/AEQ/mo256714.htm (accessed 26 March 2012).

3 The students: too valuable to fail

1 Ft. 25 in Buser. William Deresiewicz, "Solitude and Leadership", *The American Scholar* (Spring 2010), p. 4.

2 "The Creativity Conundrum,"/ *luce.net/*, Winter/Spring 2012, http://www.usnwc.edu/Lucent/OpenPdf.aspx?id=110&Title=Creativity (accessed 27 March 2012).

3 Admiral James Stavridis, "Professionals Write", *Marine Corps Gazette*, May 2011, p.83.

4 Hughes, p. 154.

5 War College students, like students everywhere, share information on courses. For example, a 2001 email post from "Airborne Ranger" on a website shares information about the Army War College, including: "War College is also one year long…No one is ever failed from it," http://www.degreeinfo.com/general-distance-learning-discussions/2561-need-info-army-war-college-please.html (accessed 31 March 2012).

6   Jospf, commenting at: http://ricks.foreignpolicy.com/posts/2012/04/19/general_scales_roasts_pme#commentspace (accessed 21 April 2012).

7   http://www.usnwc.edu/About/Fast-Facts.aspx (accessed 20 March 2012).

8   http://www.au.af.mil/au/awc/awchome.htm (accessed 20 March 2012).

9   The Naval War College was accredited, in 1984, http://www.usnwc.edu/Academics/College-of-Distance-Education/Frequently-Asked-Questions.aspx (accessed 31 March 2012). The National War College was accredited in 1993. http://www.ndu.edu/info/history.cfm (accessed 31 March 2012). The Army War College was accredited in 2004, Tom Zimmerman, "USAWC Receives Academic Accreditation," *Carlisle Banner*, 28 June 2004, http://www.carlisle.army.mil/banner/archives/2004_6.html (accessed 31 March 2012). The Air War College was also accredited in 2004, http://www.au.af.mil/au/cf/au_catalog/au_catalog.pdf (accessed 31 March 2012).

10   Cynthia Watson discusses Goldwater-Nichols specifically wanting to bring the Navy in line with the other services regarding education because the Navy "did not value the classroom" and the attitude that "'school house' discussions could never match the education provided by being out on deployment with the fleet," *Military Education,* 2007, p. 15.

11   Correspondence with the author from Wayne A. Silkett, Lieutenant Colonel (retired), 19 March 2012. Professor Silkett was an Army War College faculty member from 1989 to 2005.

12   Robert Scales, "Too Busy to Learn," *Proceedings,* February 2010, http://www.usni.org/magazines/proceedings/2010-02/too-busy-learn (accessed 26 March 2012).

13   Maxwell, p. 3.

14   The military tends to mimic the business sector in its use of annoying terms like "thinking outside the box." See Max Mallett, Brett Nelson, and Chris Steiner, "The Most Annoying, Pretentious and Useless Business Jargon", *Forbes*, 30 January 2012. http://finance.yahoo.com/news/the-most-annoying–pretentious-and-useless-business-jargon.html?mod=pf-series-a-article (accessed 26 March 2012).

15   "America's Last ICBM*,"* *The Wright Stuff*, 19 February 2009.

16   "America's Indispensable ICBM Force," http://www.docstoc.com/docs/86841578/Americas-Indispensable-ICBM-Force (accessed 26 March 2012).

17   http://www.usna.edu/EnglishDept/ (accessed 12 December 2011). There are many issues regarding how best to prepare military officers at the undergraduate level as well. There seems a current interest in perhaps even closing the service academies and opting for a British Sandhurst approach or expanding ROTC programs. These are mportant issues that are beyond the scope of this examination. See Charity E. Winters, "Now Hear This: Why Service Academies Matter," *Proceedings Magazine*, February 2012.

18   Father James Schall, "What a Student Owes His Teacher," http://www.catholiceducation.org/articles/education/ed0003.html (accessed 28 March 2012).

19   Ibid.

20   Wiarda, p. 69.

21   Hughes, p. 154.
22   Referencing the title of Adam Ross Sorkin's book, *Too Big to Fail: The Inside Story of How Wall Street and Washington Fought to Save the Financial System – and Themselves*, Viking Books, 2009.
23   Scott Bethel, Aaron Prupas, Tomisalv Ruby, and Michael Smith, "Developing Air Force Strategists: Change Culture, Reverse Careerism," *Joint Forces Quarterly*, 58, 3 (2010), 82–88.

4   Faculty: but not necessarily in a collegial sense

1   John P. Frazee, "Why Can't We Just Get Along," *Chronicle of Higher Education*, 1 April 2008, http://chronicle.com/article/Why-We-Cant-Just-Get-Along/45742/ (accessed 27 March 2012).
2   This is a case where urban legend was correct. Judith Stiehm states, regarding the Naval War College, "Seven core faculty have 'indefinite appointments'," and references the Naval War College 1994 Self Study, pp. 35, 37. (Stiehm, p. 13).
3   Hughes, p. 157.
4   Wiarda, p. 109.
5   The FPRI event triggered several iterations of discussion in the blogosphere. An audio file of the event is available at the FPRI website. See "The Future of Professional Military Education", sponsored by the Foreign Policy Research Institute and the Reserve Officer Association, Washington, D.C., 18 April 2012, http://www.fpri.org/multimedia/2012/20120418.symposium.militaryeducation.html (accessed 20 April 2012); see also Tom Nichols, "The Future of Professional Military Education," *The War Room*, http://tomnichols.net/ blog/ 2012/04/20/the-future-of-professional-military-education/ (accessed 20 April 2012); Robert Scales, "Slightly 'steamed,' Gen. Scales explains his criticism of the military's war colleges," *The Best Defense*, 11 May 2012, http://ricks.foreignpolicy.com/posts/2012/05/11/slightly_steamed_gen_scales_ explains_his_criticism_of_the_militarys_war_colleges (accessed 11 May 2012); Tom Nichols, "General Scales, Civilian Academics and Military Education," *The War Room*, 13 May 2012, http://tomnichols.net/blog/2012/ 05/13/general-scales-civilian-academics-and-military-education/ (accessed 13 May 2012).
6   Reed, p. 2.
7   Reed, p. 3.
8   The 1980 Bayh-Dole Act allowed scientists conducting federally funded research to retain patents on any inventions they create as a result of that research. See: Information on the Government's Right to Assert Ownership Control over Federally Funded Inventions, GAO-09-742, 27 July, 2009, http://www.gao.gov/products/GAO-09-742 (accessed 27 March 2012).
9   Thomas P.M. Barnett, *The Pentagon's New Map: War and Peace in the 21st Century*, Putnam Books, 2004.
10   http://thomaspmbarnett.com/new-map-journal/2004/3/27/preface-to-the-pentagons-new-map.html (accessed 31 March 2012).

11   Thomas Barnett's 24 December 2004 blog post including discussion about the institutional approval he believed he had for his activities has been reposted at http://www.freerepublic.com/focus/f-news/1310512/posts (accessed 27 March 2012).

12   His letter of resignation is posted on his blog, http://thomaspmbarnett.com/blueprint-journal/2005/1/3/letter-of-resignation-submitted-to-naval-war-college.html (accessed 27 March 2012).

13   "Old Man in a Hurry," July 2005.

14   James P. Wisecup, "President's Forum," *Naval War College Review*, Summer 2011.

15   Harper Perennial, 1998

16   James Clay Moltz, "Asia's Space Race," (New York: Columbia University Press, 2012), p. vlll.

17   Janeen Klinger, "Academics and Professional Military Education," *Academic Exchange Quarterly*, Summer 2004, 8, 2, http://www.higher-ed.org/AEQ/mo256714.htm (accessed 27 March 2012).

18   Thomas Bruscino, "Naval Gazing Google Deep: The Expertise Gap in the Academic–Military Relationship," in Douglas Higbee (ed.) *Military Culture and Education* (Ashgate, 2010), p. 141.

19   Lt. Col. Mark McCann, "Faculty Deployments Strengthen Curriculum, Validate Classroom Concepts," *Army War College Community Banner*, 26 January 2012, http://www.carlisle.army.mil/banner/article.cfm?id=2344 (accessed 27 March 2012).

20   Military sociologist Charles C. Moskos initially used the institutional and occupational professional models in conjunction with the military. See "From Institutions to Occupation: Trends in Military Organization," *Armed Forces & Society*, 1977, 4: 41–50; "Institutional and Occupational Trends in Armed Forces," in Charles C. Moskos and Frank R. Wood (eds.) *The Military: More than just a job?* (London: Pergamon-Brassey's International Defense Publishers, 1998).

21   Todd Harrison, Analysis of the FY 2012 Defense Budget, Center for Strategic and Budgetary Analysis, p. 29.

22   Called "Field Studies" at the National War College, http://www.ndu.edu/nwc/academics/FieldStudies.cfm (accessed 23 March 2012); Howard Wiarda discusses the NDU regional trips he participated on in his book. See Chapter 5.

23   Regional field studies at the Air War College are described as part of the curriculum at http://www.au.af.mil/au/awc/curriculum.htm (accessed 4 August 2012).

24   Hughes, p. 155.

25   Dr. Janeen Klinger provides percentage figures of PME faculty with prior military experience in her 2004 article "Academics and Professional Military Education," but no information is provided on how or where those percentages were obtained. *Academic Exchange Quarterly*, Summer 2004, 8, 2, http://www.higher-ed.org/AEQ/mo256714.htm (accessed 27 March 2012).

26 See Gordon Adams and Matthew Leatherman, "A Leaner and Meaner Defense: "How to Cut the Pentagon's Budget while Improving its Performance," *Foreign Affairs*, Jan/Feb 2011, 90, 1, 152–154; James Dao and Mary Williams Walsh, "Retiree Benefits for the Military could Face Cuts," *New York Times*, 19 September 2011; Baker Spring, "Time to Meet the Challenge of Updating the Military Retirement System," WebMemo, The Heritage Foundation, No. 3378, 29 September 2011. For the military's side of the argument, see a *New York Times* editorial written by three active-duty Army lieutenant-colonels. Darrell Driver, Jin Pak, and Kyle Jette, "Don't Go after Military Pensions," 27 December 2011. Similarly, after a former top Navy and DOD official spoke to Naval War College students in 2012 about approaching "tough times" for the Pentagon budget, and the impact on national security, the follow-up question from the audience was about military pensions.

27 Hughes, p. 150.

28 Reed, p. 4.

29 Reed, p. 4.

30 Reed, p. 4.

31 See the opinion of Judge JoAnn Ruggerio in Tim Bakken v. Department of the Army, U.S. Merit Protections Systems Board, New York Field Office, Docket Number NY 1221-12-0041-W-1, 6 July 6 2012. The Court's decision is subject to appeal. A similar case was raised a year earlier at the U.S. Air Force Academy, when Professor David Mullin claimed he was retaliated against for claiming that the Air Force Academy's leadership was inflating the qualifications of its faculty. A subsequent investigation substantiated Mullin's claim and found Academy leaders "negligent" in their duties. Mullin's contract was not renewed, and his civil case is still in progress. See Tom Nichols, "The Air Force Academy investigation and the current state of military education," *The War Room*, 4 July 2012, http://tomnichols.net/blog/2012/07/04/air-force-academy-investigation-current-state-military-education/ (accessed 13 July 2012).

32 http://www.usnwc.edu/About/Fast-Facts.aspx (accessed 2 April 2012).

33 http://www.usnwc.edu/About/Fast-Facts.aspx (accessed 2 April 2012).

34 http://www.usnwc.edu/About/Fast-Facts.aspx (accessed 2 April 2012).

35 This is a common mantra at PME institutions, which I have encountered at both the Air and Naval War Colleges; for a similar description of National, see Wiarda, pp. 67–68.

36 Hughes, 2010, pp. 150–151.

37 Naval War College Professor Bradford Lee discusses the evolution of faculty recruitment in the Strategy & Policy (S&P) Department. He states that a number of issues "have made it hard for us in recent years to recruit mid-career civilian professors who have both the educational background and the intellectual adaptability to add immediate value to the Strategy and Policy curriculum. Changing our recruitment strategy yet again, we have shifted our focus to younger scholars who have just finished their doctoral dissertations..." How well the students accept these younger scholars is difficult to determine however. According to the data Professor Lee provides, S&P utilizes teaching teams that are evaluated jointly, rather than individually.

Bradford A. Lee, "Teaching Strategy: A Scenic View from Newport," in Gabriel Marcella (ed.) *Teaching Strategy: Challenge and Response*, US Army Strategic Studies Institute, 2010, pp. 112–114.

38 http://www.jbhe.com/2012/01/us-naval-war-college-maritime-history-professor/ (accessed 27 March 2012).

39 Wiarda, p. 72.

40 Steeljaw Scribe, "Does Keeping PME Relevant Mean Fixing the Faculty First?" USNI Blog, 14 August 2011, http://blog.usni.org/2011/08/14/does-keeping-pme-relevant-mean-fixing-the-faulty-first/ (accessed 27 March 2012).

41 Watson, 2010, p. 151.

42 Wiarda, p. 35.

43 Discussion about problems on this issue at the National Defense University have been prominent lately. See: Tom Ricks, "Continuing Erosion at NDU," *The Best Defense*, 14 June 2012, http://ricks.foreignpolicy.com/posts/2012/06/14/continuing_erosion_at_ndu (accessed 4 August 2012); Robert Goldrich, "NDU: In Worse Shape than Tom Thinks," *The Best Defense*," 15 June 2012, http://ricks.foreignpolicy.com/posts/2012/06/15/ndu_in_worse_shape_than_tom_thinks (accessed 4 August 2012); "Guest Post by Joan Johnson-Freese: An Update on Professional Military Education." *USNI Blog*, 3 July 2012. http://blog.usni.org/2012/07/03/guest-post-by-joan-johnson-freese-an-update-on-profession-military-education/ (accessed 4 August 2012).

44 Tom Ricks recently commented about leadership issues at NDU. "Part of the problem with the place, is that the generals and admirals overseeing the place don't know much about how to run a university, and wouldn't know intellectual firepower from a day-old dud." "Continuing Erosion at NDU," *The Best Defense*, 14 June 2012, http://ricks.foreignpolicy.com/posts/2012/06/14/continuing_erosion_at_ndu (accessed 4 August 2012).

45 Wiarda, p. 28.

46 Reed, p. 5.

47 Stiehm, pp. 19–20.

48 Carl Elliott, "Meddle Management," *The Wall Street Journal*, 2 September 2011.

49 http://www.politifact.com/truth-o-meter/statements/2011/nov/14/newt-gingrich/newt-gingrich-says-2014-there-will-be-one-administ/ (accessed 31 March 2012).

50 *Naval War College Faculty Handbook*, 2007, p.33 (electronic version available on NWC intranet only) (accessed 2 April 2012).

51 Hughes, p. 151.

5 The curriculum: moving toward intellectual agility

1 Dave Maxwell, "Thoughts on Professional Military Education: After 9-11, Iraq, and Afghanistan in the Era of Fiscal Austerity, 1 January 2012.

2 Officer Professional Military Education Policy, CJCSI 1800.01, 15 July 2009,

http://www.dtic.mil/cjcs_directives/cdata/unlimit/1800_01.pdf (accessed 27 March 2012).

3   Officer Professional Military Education Policy, CJCSI 1800.01, 15 July 2009, Appendix E, http://www.dtic.mil/cjcs_directives/cdata/unlimit/1800_01.pdf (accessed 5 April 2012).

4   Naval War College self study, submitted to CJCS PAJE Team for JPME Phase 2, May 2009, pp. 4–40.

5   See Bloom's Taxonomy of Cognitive Domain, http://classweb.gmu.edu/ndabbagh/Resources/Resources2/bloomstax.htm (accessed 27 March 2012).

6   Mark Moyer, "Counterinsurgency and Professional Military Education," *Small Wars Journal*, 2009. http://smallwarsjournal.com/blog/journal/docs-temp/329-moyar.pdf (accessed 27 March 2012).

7   Wiarda, p. 43.

8   Hughes, p. 155.

9   James Schneider, "And Another Thing, Military Strategic Education is Far Worse than Tom Thinks," *Best Defense*, 22 June 2011, http://ricks.foreignpolicy.com/posts/2011/06/22/and_another_thing_military_strategic_education_is_far_worse_than_tom_thinks (accessed 27 March 2012).

10 Cited in "Does Keeping PME Relevant Mean Fixing the Faculty First?" USNI Blog, 14 August 2011.

11 "Keeping PME Relevant...It's a Military Problem," 5 August 2011, USNI Blog, http://blog.usni.org/2011/12/05/keeping-pme-relevant-%E2%80%93-it%E2%80%99s-a-military-problem%E2%80%A6/ (accessed 27 March 2012).

12 Watson, *Teaching Strategy*, 2010, p. 160.

13 Lee, *Teaching Strategy*, 2010, p. 112.

14 Correspondence to the author from Wayne A. Silkett, Lieutenant Colonel (retired), 19 March 2012. Professor Silkett was an Army War College faculty member from 1989 to 2005.

15 Stiehm, p. 199.

16 Problems can certainly arise in civilian academia as well. See Dan Berrett, "Academic Freedom and Holocaust Denial," *Inside Higher Ed*, 26 October 2010, http://www.insidehighered.com/news/2010/10/26/siddique

17 Noah Shachtman and Spencer Ackerman, "US Military Taught Officers: Use "Hiroshima "Tactics for "total War" on Islam," 10 May 2012, http://www.wired.com/dangerroom/tag/joint-forces-staff-college/ (accessed 11 May 2012).

18 Pauline Jelinek and Robert Burns, "Joint Forces Staff College Class Suspended after Teaching America's Enemy is Islam," *Huffington Post*, 11 May 2012.

19 "Pentagon condemns "war on Islam" US training class, BBC News, 11 May 2012, http://www.bbc.co.uk/news/world-us-canada-18032968 (accessed 11 May 2012).

20 http://www.carlisle.army.mil/banner/article.cfm?id=1365 (accessed 27 March 2012).

21 Dan Hughes, pp. 160–161.

22 Naval War College Self Study submitted to CJCS PAJE Team for JPME Phase 2, April 2009, pp. 4-39, 4-42, 4-43, 4-46,

23 Andrew Gillen, Daniel L. Bennett and Richard Vedder, "The Inmates Running the Asylum? An Analysis of Higher Education Accreditation," Center for College Affordability and Productivity, October 2010, http://www.centerfor-collegeaffordability.org/uploads/Accreditation.pdf (accessed 27 March 2012).

24 Gillen, Bennett and Vedder, p. 3.

25 http://www.usnwc.edu/Academics/College-of-Distance-Education/Frequently-Asked-Questions.aspx (accessed 27 March 2012).

26 Janeen Klinger wrote in 2004 that "the shift from military training to graduate level rigor is relatively new to PME institutions." "Academics and Professional Military Education," *Academic Exchange Quarterly*, Summer 2004, Volume 8, Issue 2. http://www.higher-ed.org/AEQ/mo256714.htm (accessed 27 March 2012). It is Goldwater-Nichols that has imposed that expected rigor, not accreditation.

27 Mr. Skelton continues to champion Civil-Military issues since leaving office, writing on the topic. "The Civil-Military Gap Need Not Become a Challenge," *Joint Forces Quarterly*, 64, 1st Quarter, 2012, 60–66. He says: "A difference in values, knowledge, and experience between the military and society is inherent in the system and is not detrimental in itself. However, if the military and society move further apart, that could have grave consequences for the military as the two sides struggle to communicate and understand each other... There is a civil-military gap that is serious and growing...Both the military and society have contributed to its creation and expansion, and both have a responsibility to work to narrow it" (p. 61). He then goes on to discuss where responsibility lies for addressing the issues in the military: "Commissioned and noncommissioned officers set the tone for subordinate commanders and troops. This is an important but too often neglected dimension of the command climate. These officers improve the command through the examples they set" (pp. 63–64).

28 Representative Steve Israel (D-NY) sponsored a PME conference in 2006, Rebuilding America's Intellectual Arsenal, focussing on linguistic and cultural capabilities, http://smallwarsjournal.com/documents/housepmeconference.pdf (accessed 27 March 2012).

29 This comment was made to an NWC faculty member during a conference on War College teaching methods in 2003.

30 The expanse of the fiefdoms continues to grow. The National Defense University, College of International Security Affairs, includes a branch at Fort Bragg, NC, which offers a Master's degree in Strategic Studies. In 2012, even with federal government fiscal constraints looming, NDU advertised through the Inter-University Seminar on Armed Forces and Society for three new faculty positions at the Assistant and Associate level to teach "subjects related to the challenges of the contemporary international security environment," with a salary range of $85,000–$115,000. The average faculty salary for Assistant Professors in the social sciences in civilian academia was approximately $59,000 in 2011; $69,000 for Associates, and lower for history faculty. *National Faculty Salary Survey*, College and University Professional

Association for Human Resources, 2011, http://www.cupahr.org/surveys/files/salary2011/NFSS11ExecutiveSummary.pdf (accessed 27 March 2012)

31 Watson, *Military Education*, 2007, p. 15.

6 Recommendations and conclusion

1 Correspondence to the author, 19 March 2012.

2 http://ricks.foreignpolicy.com/posts/2012/04/24/what_exactly_did_tom_say_about_military_education_at_last_week_s_fpri_hoedown (accessed 11 May 2012).

3 McArdle, "Why Companies Fail," *The Atlantic*, March 2012, p. 32, http://www.theatlantic.com/magazine/archive/2012/03/why-companies-fail/8887/ (accessed 27 March 2012).

4 Robert Goldich, "Sure, introduce more rigor into the professional military education system, but not by imitating civilian schools," *The Best Defense*, 3 May 2012, http://ricks.foreignpolicy.com/posts/2012/05/03/sure_introduce_more_rigor_into_the_professional_military_education_system_but_not_b (accessed 11 May 2012).

5 Stiehm, p. 199.

6 Thomas Mahnken, "What's Right and What's Wrong: The Two Faces of the Pacific Pivot," 30 December 2011, http://shadow.foreignpolicy.com/blog/5630 (accessed 27 March 2012); Thomas Mahnken, "A Risky Defense Strategy," 5 January 2012, http://shadow.foreignpolicy.com/posts/2012/01/05/a_risky_defense_strategy (accessed 27 March 2012).

7 http://www.aaup.org/AAUP/pubsres/policydocs/contents/1940statement.htm (accessed 27 March 2012).

8 "Seeing Crimson," *The Economist*, 3 January 2002, www.economist.com/node/923104 (accessed 27 March 2012).

9 General Martin Dempsey, USA, Chairman Joint Chiefs of Staff, Joint Education White Paper, 16 July 2012. http://www.jcs.mil//content/files/2012-07/071812110954_CJCS_Joint_Education_White_Paper.pdf (accessed 21 July 2012).

10 Stephen B. Luce, Rear Admiral, U.S. Navy, address delivered at the U.S. Naval War College (2 June 1903), quoted in John D. Hayes and John B. Hattendorf (eds.) *The Writings of Stephen B. Luce* (Newport, RI: Naval War College, 1975), pp. 39–40.

Select bibliography

Allen, Charles, "Redress of Military Education: The Clarion Call," *Joint Forces Quarterly*, Fall 2010.

Bethel, Scott, Aaron Prupas, Tomisalv Ruby, and Michael Smith, "Developing Air Force Strategists: Change Culture, Reverse Careerism," *Joint Forces Quarterly*, 58, 3, 2010, pp. 82–88.

Bruscino, Thomas, "Naval Gazing Google Deep: The Expertise Gap in the Academic–Military Relationship," in Douglas Higbee (ed.) *Military Culture and Education* (Aldershot: Ashgate, 2010).

Fleming, Bruce, *Annapolis Autumn: Life, Death, and Literature at the U.S. Naval Academy* (New York: New Press, 2005).

Frazee, John P., "Why Can't We just Get Along," *Chronicle of Higher Education*, online posting, 1 April 2008, available at http://chronicle.com/article/Why-We-Cant-Just-Get-Along/45742/ (accessed 27 March 2012).

Frerichs, Rebecca L. and Stephen R. DiRienzo, "Establishing a Framework for Intelligence Education and Training, *Joint Forces Quarterly*, 62, 3rd quarter 2011, 70–71.

Gillen, Andrew, Daniel L. Bennett, and Richard Vedder, "The Inmates Running the Asylum? An Analysis of Higher Education Accreditation," Center for College Affordability and Productivity, October 2010, online posting, available at http://www.centerforcollegeaffordability.org/uploads/Accreditation.pdf (accessed 27 March 2012).

Hughes, Daniel, "Professors in the Colonels' World," in Douglas Higbee (ed.) *Military Culture and Education* (Burlington, VT: Ashgate, 2010).

Huntington, Samuel, *The Soldier and the State: The Theory and Politics of Civil–Military Relations* (Cambridge, MA: Belknap Press, 1981).

Kilger, Janeen, "Academics and Professional Military Education," *Academic Exchange Quarterly*, Summer 2004, 8, 2, online posting, available at http://www.higher-ed.org/AEQ/mo2567l4.htm (accessed 26 March 2012).

McMaster, H.R., *Dereliction of Duty: Johnson, McNamara, the Joint Chiefs of Staff, and the Lies that Led to Vietnam* (Harper Perennial, 1998).

Mazur, Diane H., *A More Perfect Military: How the Constitution Can Make Our Military Stronger* (Oxford: Oxford University Press, 2010).

Moskos, Charles C., "From Institutions to Occupation: Trends in Military

Organization," *Armed Forces & Society*, 1977, 4, 41–50.

Moyer, Mark, "Counterinsurgency and Professional Military Education," *Small Wars Journal*, online posting, 2009, available at http://smallwarsjournal.com/blog/journal/docs-temp/329-moyar.pdf (accessed 27 March 2012)

Owens, Mackubin Thomas, "Lessons Learned," *National Review Online*, online posting, 7 August 2006, available at http://www.nationalreview.com/nrd/article/?q=NDk3YmEwN2Y5OTg4NTZmNzhjOTTdmYTRjYzEyNGFjY2M= (accessed 26 March 2012).

Peters, Ralph, "Learning to Lose," *The American Interest*, July–August 2007, http://www.the-american-interest.com/article.cfm?piece=291 (accessed 26 March 2012).

Petraeus, David H., "Beyond the Cloister," *The American Interest*, July–August 2007, online posting, available at http://www.the-american-interest.com/article.cfm?piece=290 (accessed 26 March 2012).

Reed, George E., "What's Wrong and What's Right with the War Colleges," *DefensePolicy.Org*, online posting, 1 July 2011, available at http://www.defensepolicy.org/2011/george-reed/what%E2%80%99s-wrong-and-right-with-the-war-colleges (accessed 26 March 2012).

Ricks, Tom, "Need Budget Cuts? We Can Probably Start by Shutting Down the Air War College," *The Best Defense,* online posting, 11 April 2011, available at http://ricks.foreignpolicy.com/posts/2011/04/11/need_budget_cuts_we_probably_can_start_by_shutting_the_air_war_college (accessed 26 March 2012).

Scales, Robert H. "Too Busy to Learn?" *Proceedings*, February 2010.

Stavridis, James, "Read…Think…and Write," 15 August 2011, online posting, available at http://www.aco.nato.int/saceur/read-think-write.aspx (accessed 26 March 2012).

Steele, William M. and Robert Kupiszewski, "Joint Education: Where Do We Go from Here?" *Joint Forces Quarterly*, Winter 1993–94, 63–70.

Stiehm, Judith Hick, *The U.S. Army War College: Military Education in a Democracy* (Philadelphia, PA: Temple University Press, 2002).

Watson, Cynthia A. *Military Education: A Reference Handbook* (Westport, CT: Praeger, 2007).

Watts, Barry, Center for Strategic and Budgetary Assessment, "U.S. Combat Training, Operational Art and Strategic Competence: Problems and Opportunities," 2008, online posting, available at http://www.csbaonline.org/wp-content/uploads/2011/02/2008.08.21-Combat-Training-Operational-Art-Strategic-Competence.pdf (accessed 26 March 2012).

Wiarda, Howard, *Military Brass versus Civilian Academics at the National War College: Clash of Cultures* (Lanham, MD: Lexington Books, 2011).

Wisecup, James P., "President's Forum," *Naval War College Review*, Summer 2011.

Index